OCD
ADHD
Tourette Syndrome

This is an IndieMosh book
brought to you by MoshPit Publishing
an imprint of Mosher's Business Support Pty Ltd

PO Box 4363
Penrith NSW 2750

indiemosh.com.au

Copyright © Geoff Kanofski 2023 at www.geoffkanofski.com

The moral right of the author has been asserted in accordance with the Copyright Amendment (Moral Rights) Act 2000.

All rights reserved. Except as permitted under the Australian Copyright Act 1968 (for example, fair dealing for the purposes of study, research, criticism or review) no part of this publication may be reproduced, stored in a retrieval system, or transmitted in any form or by any means, electronic, mechanical, photocopying, recording or otherwise, without the written permission of the publisher.

 A catalogue record for this work is available from the National Library of Australia

https://www.nla.gov.au/collections

Title:	OCD, ADHD, Tourette Syndrome
Subtitle:	A sufferer's discovery of how these disorders are functionally linked
Author:	Kanofski, Geoff
ISBNs:	9781923065581 (paperback) 9781923065598 (ebook – epub) 9781923065604 (ebook – Kindle)
Subjects:	SELF-HELP/Compulsive Behavior/Obsessive Compulsive Disorder (OCD); PSYCHOLOGY/Psychopathology/Attention-Deficit Disorder (ADD-ADHD); BIOGRAPHY& AUTOBIOGRAPHY/People with Disabilities; PHILOSOPHY/Zen

Cover concept by Geoff Kanofski
Cover design and layout by Ally Mosher at allymosher.com

OCD
ADHD
Tourette Syndrome

A sufferer's discovery of
how these disorders
are functionally linked

Geoff Kanofski

Disclaimer

This book is a memoir. It reflects the author's recollections of experiences over time. The author is not a qualified professional. He has included views that may not have been formally researched. Therefore, the content in this book does not constitute professional advice. Some of the names of the characters have been changed for privacy reasons. The author and publisher accept no liability for any loss, damage or disruption incurred by the reader or any other person arising from any action taken or not taken based on the content of this book.

One-Page Summary

As a child, I had obsessive tendencies, poor concentration, and Tourette's tics. My performance at school was poor. I started work when I was 15 years old and my performance was still poor. At age 17, I was being tortured by obsessive-compulsive disorder.

At age 33, I discovered how all my disorders were functionally linked. This was the beginning of my understanding. I then began to overcome my OCD, which further increased my understanding of this link.

At age 35, I was no longer tortured by OCD symptoms. I began full-time study. I completed two pre-tertiary courses with hard work and tutoring. Then disability concessions enabled me to complete an Undergraduate Degree in Psychology. Eight years of full-time study helped to extend my personal understanding of this functional link.

At age 43, I was excited about working in human services. However, poor concentration caused me to fail. I tried labouring jobs, and poor concentration caused more failure. Hence, there were no disability concessions in the workplace. More activities dropped out of my life. I was now a hyperactive person without activity. I began to suffer with episodes of anger and sadness.

Understanding how my brain worked did not help my state of mind. My episodes of anger and sadness continued for a long time.

At age 55, I began to practise meditation. And meditation slowly healed my mind.

At age 64, I finished writing this book.

Contents

One-Page Summary v

1. Lockyer Valley Rain 1
2. I Pursued an Intense Lifestyle and Didn't Learn Much 5
3. Going hard in an Uncharted World 9
4. Finding a Life Outside Boxing 19
5. I Felt Physically Insurmountable 23
6. The Church, Polly, Family and Leaving the Railways 27
7. Studying 30
8. A Clear Path 37
9. Back to Boxing and then Rejections 42
10. I Found My Niche 53
11. Jail 58
12. Coaching the Boys for Boxing 65
13. What Could I Do to Occupy My Mind? 74
14. Attention Diverted to a Higher Dimension 86
15. Attention Diverted to a Higher Dimension and To Stillness 96

Appendix A. Obsessive-Compulsive Disorder (OCD) 102

Appendix B. Attention Deficit Hyperactivity Disorder (ADHD) 105

Appendix C. Tourette Syndrome (TS) 108

Appendix D. Tips for Practising Presence 110

Chapter 1

Lockyer Valley Rain

Age: Birth to 15

I was born in 1959 in a small Australian town called Laidley. My parents and I lived with my grandfather. We reared chickens and ducks and sold them to people as food. One day I heard my grandfather talking to my father about some ducklings. My grandfather said, "I'll pour the feed into these little ducks so they'll be ready for Christmas." After hearing their conversation, I caught the ducklings and pushed food down their necks with a stick and killed them all. This behaviour was primarily due to an obsessive tendency. I was obsessive about nurturing the ducklings. I wanted to make them grow extremely fast. I remember having obsessive thoughts about various things.

My obsessive tendencies were related to extreme discipline. I remember my parents were shopping in the city, and they bought me a toy car. I remember holding this toy car on the handrail of an escalator, which made the wheels go around. I asked my parents to finish their shopping while I stood at the bottom of the escalator and held the toy on the moving handrail. I stood there for hours making the wheels go around. I was about five years old. I applied extreme discipline to carry out this activity for such a long time. This is an example of how my obsessive tendencies were related to extreme discipline.

I also experienced repetitive thinking activities. I recall lying on my back and looking up at the sky. I wondered how far the sky went. I wondered how everything came into existence. I wondered if God made it. And I wondered how God came to exist. I thought about these things over and over again.

I remember being lonely when I was a small child, as I didn't have brothers or sisters. However, my loneliness was somewhat quenched when I started school. I went to a Catholic school because it was close to where we lived. My impression of school was typical of a hyperactive child: the classroom was boring, and the schoolyard was fun.

I remember having a fuzzy perception of physical limitations. That is, I believed I could always try harder. For example, I believed I could run faster if I tried harder. I remember testing this theory when I was running around the schoolyard. I was running extremely hard (with an effort I couldn't label) and my forehead hit a thick tree branch. I was taken to hospital because I had a giant lump on my forehead. This fuzzy perception of physical limitation remained in my psyche.

I always wanted to achieve good marks at school, but I'd daydream and fail to understand the lessons. In those days, students received class placings to reflect their academic achievement: first, second, third, etc. I usually came fifteenth in a class of 17 students.

I left the Catholic school after year four and went to the state school. My first experience at this new school involved running. My peers noticed that I was a fast runner. However, my speed wasn't outstanding. I was a lot better at maintaining my speed over longer distances. I started running in 800-metre races in year six, and I'd win by 200 metres. A professional runner saw my potential and began coaching me. I joined an athletics club and began inter-club competitions. I came second in the state titles for 800 metres. My coach then discovered my ability to run longer distance races. There were no long-distance races for my age group, but world records did exist for those age groups. My coach suggested that I run in a 10,000-metre race against adults. I did that on a hot day and broke the world record for a 12-year-old. This was another example of my extreme discipline.

It was around this time that I experienced discomfort in my fingertips, and I began squeezing them. The urge to squeeze my fingertips was very strong. I could not resist doing it. It was a very stressful experience.

I was still 12 years old when my coach organised an athletics carnival in Laidley. My coach created a three-mile race because he knew I'd break another world record, and I did.

My coach left Laidley at the end of that year, and I stopped running. I then became interested in rearing turkeys. The turkeys had a three-course meal twice a day. They had grass, turkey pellets and throw-away bread from the baker. My grandfather was amazed because my turkeys grew so fast. I was obsessed with making them grow fast.

I was feeding my turkeys one morning when I was startled by the sound of a dog yelping. I ran to the roadside and saw that my dog had been hit by a car. My dog's name was Yip. Yip couldn't move her back legs after that day. The vet advised us to wait and see if she got better. Time went by and Yip never regained the use of her back legs. I remember leaving Yip in a dark room by herself because she couldn't follow me around. She eventually died. I then realised something horrible: I had neglected her. I was 13 years old.

I remember having dreams about shooting sick animals to stop them from suffering. They were horrible dreams because the animals would not die after I shot them. These dreams became more horrible because I'd realise the animals would have recovered. In other words, it wasn't necessary to shoot them at all. Now they were suffering even more. The dreams always unfolded like this.

I eventually stopped having these dreams. I'm not sure why they stopped, but I do know I became brutally honest with myself – in an obsessive-compulsive disorder (OCD) kind of way. I don't know if this caused my dreams to stop but this brutal honesty continued.

Although I had various undiagnosed symptoms, my later childhood was enjoyable. I could roam the countryside with my friends, and we rode our pushbikes for miles. We hunted wild game, and we fished in the gullies and creeks. Floods were an exciting part of my childhood. The Laidley Creek started high in the Lockyer Valley and ran 26 miles through a farming community before it reached our town. Town's people would ring the farmers on public phones to get a report on flood waters. The news in town would then spread from house to house. I remember someone saying, "A four-foot wall of water just hit the Mulgowie Bridge!" Some floods came fast, and some came slow. Some came from the creek, and others came from adjoining lagoons. It was wonderful to live in a country town in the early 1970s. If perfect happiness was a 10, I think my later childhood would have been an **8**.

I was now 15 years old and in my tenth year of school. I was always a low-achieving student. However, I was intelligent in a certain way. I recall doing a science examination in year 10. I could only answer one question in this examination. It turned out to be the hardest question on the paper, and I was the only student that answered it correctly. I left school with a year 10 certificate, recording 18 out of 45 marks.

Chapter 2

I Pursued an Intense Lifestyle and Didn't Learn Much

Age: 15 to 20

I was now excited about getting a job. Jobs were easy to get in the mid-1970s. My father wanted me to apply for an apprenticeship at the Ipswich Railway Workshops. I didn't know much about anything, so I just did what my father wanted me to do.

I started work at the railway workshops as an apprentice boilermaker. This was the beginning of a very different life. I travelled from Laidley to Ipswich with some colleagues who worked in the workshops. I got up early and came home late. I'd go to rugby league training when I got home from work. That perked me up. After training, I'd go into town and play snooker. I'd come home when the snooker shop closed, and my father would get out of bed and reprimand me for going to bed too late. However, he believed I was an adult because I was now working. Therefore, he just expressed his concern and went back to bed.

Sleep deprivation did make me suffer at work, especially when I wasn't busy. I wasn't happy in the railway workshops, but I continued to work there because people said

I should. My average happiness dropped from 8 to **6**.

I didn't socialise at work. A few of the lads called me "Have-A-Chat" because I didn't talk much. I'm not sure why I didn't talk much. I just dragged myself through the boring days.

Another one-and-a-half years passed by. I was now 17 years old. I began to have symptoms of OCD. I thought about things over and over again. And I'd tense my muscles and hold my breath, as I repeated these thoughts. I was straining my brain to convince myself that I thought about something. I was never sure what I had thought, or if I even *had* the thought. These compulsions tortured me, and I didn't tell anyone about it.

I then started running again. I was soon running too far and too hard. My dieting was obsessive and neurotic. I'd run 16 miles around a mountain and lose four kilograms of fluid, then drink coffee. I was always tired. My average happiness dropped from 6 to **5**.

One of my shins got sore but I kept on running. I'd run until my shin went numb. An X-ray revealed a sack of puss on my shin bone. The doctor prescribed antibiotics and told me to stop running. I had developed a neurotic passion for running, and I didn't want to stop. But I did.

My parents had bought a house in Ipswich by now. That meant I didn't need to travel from Laidley to Ipswich for work. My contact with Laidley began to fade. With that, my social life also faded. And not being able to run made everything worse. My happiness dropped to **4**.

I had another X-ray of my shin. The sack of pus had cleared, and a stress fracture was revealed. Being unable to run prompted me to do boxing training. I decided to have an amateur fight and got belted from pillar to post. But that didn't worry me too much. I just wanted an activity to occupy my mind.

My shin took three months to heal. I started running

again and tore my hamstring. It took another three months for my hamstring to heal. I then began running again and contracted a virus. The virus went away, but it left me with severe muscular stiffness. I couldn't run. I had nothing interesting to do and I was quite sad. My average happiness probably dropped to about **3**.

My muscular stiffness wouldn't get better. The doctor tested me for everything but couldn't find the cause of my muscular stiffness. He concluded that my muscular stiffness was caused by my mind. I couldn't understand how my mind could cause this. Anyway, I went to a field and ran because the doctor said I could. I ran for one minute and I fell to the ground (my legs gave away). I got up and ran again. And I ran the following day. My muscular stiffness went away, so the doctor must have been right.

I was now back into physical training. I had gained seven kilograms in nine months while I wasn't training or dieting. I trained for a few months without dieting, and I became strong. I decided to have another fight and won. I performed a lot better this time.

The experience of winning my second fight must have given me confidence. I began to express myself more. "Have-A-Chat" ceased to exist. The boys at the workshops then called me "Crazy" because I expressed myself like a crazy person. My average happiness rose quickly to **7**.

I became very passionate about boxing. I didn't have a lot of skill. My obsessive personality drove me to train hard, but I didn't restrict my food intake anymore. Fitness and durability became my attributes. The next two years were a series of bruising encounters. The boys at the workshops called me "Mince Face" because of the injuries I received. I continued to work in the railway workshops, but I didn't learn much about my work. I didn't learn much about anything. All I cared about was boxing and exercising.

I was now 19 years old, and the term of my apprenticeship had expired. I now had to pass my trade test. Passing my trade test was a difficult task. I tried several times, but I was too slow. I eventually passed because my employer was lenient.

I was now a qualified tradesman. I was placed on a production line where each tradesman had the same task to do. I was always the last to finish. I tried very hard because I didn't like being the slowest worker in the gang. For some reason, my performance was always below the normal standard.

The Ipswich Railways Workshops supported workers who lacked skills. These workers were given simple jobs to do. I was given oxy-cutting jobs, which were repetitious and simple. I was very quick at gouging flat welds. I didn't use a conventional gouging tip. I used a size-24 cutting tip and held the tip further away from the welds. Nobody knew how I did it so quickly. Interestingly, I was good at discovering alternative methods.

Everybody knew me in the workshops because of my excessive behaviour. I shadow-boxed in railway wagons, lifted steel for exercise, and I enjoyed being a clown. But I still had OCD symptoms (compulsions), which were very intense.

The compulsions would overtake me when I was working. I'd stop in the middle of a task and intensely think about the same thing over and over again. I'd be staring into space with an oxy-torch flaming in my hand. My workmates would see me doing this, and they would laugh at me because they thought I was being a clown. I once told someone that I wasn't clowning, and that person didn't believe me. I didn't bother telling anyone after that. I was being tortured by OCD, and nobody knew.

Chapter 3

Going hard in an Uncharted World

Age: 20 to 24

I enjoyed my amateur boxing career, although I can't remember a lot of it. I remember being one of three Ipswich boxers who went to a boxing event at Quilpie. Quilpie was an opal mining town in western Queensland. Jimmy Heaton was our coach, and he drove the car on this long trip. We drove late into the night before we decided to camp. We wrapped one big canvas around the four of us and slept on the ground.

We woke up when the sun shone on our twitching eyelids. We got up quickly to avoid the farts that had accumulated in our shared bed. The spinifex plants got smaller as we travelled westward. It was outback Queensland (a place I had never seen).

We arrived in Quilpie that day and attended the pre-fight weigh-in. We had our fights later that night. Many of the boxers slept in the hall that night because they had travelled long distances. The Ipswich boxers drank some alcohol and decided to go for a run. We ran further west and didn't stop until the sun rose. We stood together and waited to see through the fog that was blurring our vision. The fog soon cleared, and I saw the mysterious desert plains. It was so vast and flat—so quiet and eerie.

We were standing beside a cemetery. I felt like I was standing on top of the world.

The Amateur Boxing Association put all the boxers through a routine electroencephalogram (EEG). This was a medical test that measured the electrical activity of the brain. The test revealed an abnormality in my frontal lobe. I was then referred to a neurosurgeon who told me that I was six times more likely to have a seizure than a normal person. The neurosurgeon didn't stop me from boxing, but he recommended that I have an EEG every six months.

To make matters worse, a dentist told me that my nose would enter my brain if it was pushed back any further. I had recently suffered a broken bone, which was at the level of my eyes. The dentist's attention was drawn to the injury because I had two black eyes. I mention the words of the dentist and neurosurgeon to explain my OCD symptoms. My explanation follows.

The words of the dentist and neurosurgeon caused me to have compulsive thoughts (OCD symptoms). I tried to think of the reasons why I should continue boxing. I then tried to count all these reasons. However, I couldn't count them because I had forgotten some of them. I tried very hard to remember them all. I contracted my muscles in an effort to remember all these reasons and to count them. I eventually managed to recall all the reasons. I then tried to count the reasons again because I wasn't sure if I counted them properly. This intense thinking continued for hours. By this time, I was lying in a bed soaked with perspiration. I had to get through it; I had to recall every reason, and I had to be sure that I counted them properly. This was the only way I could justify my decision to continue boxing. I eventually got through it, but I didn't sleep that night. This is an example of my compulsive thinking about a matter that was important to me. However, I also had compulsive thoughts about matters that were *not* important. Therefore, the cause of my OCD was not easy to understand (at the time).

My OCD symptoms were extremely painful, but my average happiness remained at **7**. I think my boxing activity made me happy. I travelled to Thailand for an international boxing competition called the King's Cup. It was extremely hot in Thailand. Most of the guys in the team thought I was crazy because I went for runs in the hot sun. I didn't compete in Thailand because I sustained a cut over my eyebrow during a sparring session. I didn't pass the medical examination.

I shared a room in Thailand with another boxer. This fellow was eliminated from the competition quite early. Both of us were now out of the competition, so we decided to have a good time. There was civil hostility in Thailand at the time. Nobody was allowed to leave their hotel after dark. One night my roommate and I got drunk and wandered out of our hotel. We were wandering around Bangkok when soldiers confronted us with guns. These fellows seemed quite intense. Then we remembered the curfew. Fortunately, my roommate was a sharp thinker. He said, "King's Cup, King's Cup," and added a few gestures. The soldiers then realised that we were King's Cup competitors, and they ordered us to go back to the hotel.

The Australian boxers went to the markets in Bangkok. There were multitudes of people at these markets, and I lost contact with the team. I didn't know where I was. I approached a taxi driver, but I couldn't tell him where I was staying (I couldn't remember). Fortunately, the taxi driver made some inquiries and found out where I was staying. He then drove me to the hotel.

My experience in Thailand continued. One day the curfew was extended to daylight hours, which prevented me from having my usual run in the sun. I sprinted several times through the corridor of the hotel on that day. Our team manager wasn't happy about that. On another occasion, I went for a run and was late for the closing ceremony, which made him annoyed with me. I didn't mean to be late; I just lost track of time. I then lost my airline ticket from Sydney to Brisbane. My trainer (in Ipswich) had to contact the travel agency to get me home. So, my trip to Thailand was a failure on many accounts. I failed with various things in my life. However, my continued failure didn't worry me too much. I guess I got used to making mistakes.

My next major trip for boxing was for the President's Cup in Indonesia. This was an international boxing competition like the King's Cup. I drew a Japanese boxer for my first fight. I had a plan about how I would fight this man. However, the plan made me perform badly. I rushed at my opponent with my head down and got punished with uppercuts. My opponent got tired as the fight went on, but I was disqualified for rushing in with my head down. I was now eliminated from the competition. Being eliminated allowed me the freedom to do what I wanted to do. Therefore, I ran during the day and roamed around at night. My trip to Indonesia was exciting because I was a young man, and I was seeing the world.

I was now 21 years old. I had been keeping company with a girl for four years. Our relationship didn't have much impact on my psychological conditioning, and that's why I haven't mentioned it before now. We decided to get married, which was not an intelligent decision because we were both immature. I didn't give my wife much attention because I was too interested in boxing. I mention this relationship so that the reader can understand something I will mention later. Hence, this book is presented chronologically.

I continued to train hard and pursue my boxing career. The Amateur Boxing Association ran tournaments to decide the national champions for each year. If you won the state title, you could then represent your state at the national titles for that year. I competed in the national titles in 1980 and was beaten on points in the final. It was now time for the national titles of 1981. I decided to make this my last year in amateur boxing. Therefore, this was my last chance to win a national title.

The national titles were held over three days. I had to fight every day to win the title. I beat the New South Wales champion on the first day and the Tasmanian champion on the second day. I was now set to fight the Victorian champion in the final. The Victorian was an explosive boxer with fast-twitch muscles (the kind of muscles that sprinters have). The duration of the contest was three by three-minute rounds. Therefore, the short distance suited my opponent.

The bell rang and I attacked relentlessly. The Victorian hit me with uppercuts as I attacked. His uppercuts damaged me, but I kept coming forward. I really wanted to win the Australian national title. As usual, my opponent weakened toward the end. The Victorian ended up winning by a split decision. The medals were presented in a ceremonial fashion after the fight. We stood on a podium to receive our medals. The Victorian stood in the middle; the New South Welshman and I stood on either side. I cried while the national anthem played. I really wanted to win the Australian title.

My amateur boxing career was now finished. Failing to win the Australian title didn't bother me for long as I had other things to pursue. I didn't know if I wanted to pursue a professional boxing career or take up running. Therefore, I was happy to run and choose my goal later.

By this time, my wife and I had been married for two

years. We decided to have a baby. We had a daughter and called her Kristy. Then my wife decided to leave me, and she took Kristy with her. Kristy was just three months old.

My happiness dropped significantly because I was separated from Kristy. And I was also concerned about her safety. But this problem didn't last long. My wife had issues that prevented her from looking after Kristy, so she brought her back to me.

I now needed someone to look after Kristy while I was at work. My wife's mother (June) was happy to do this. June began caring for Kristy on a full-time basis. I visited her regularly, and everything was okay. With this, my happiness improved to **7**.

June developed a motherly attachment to Kristy. She feared that I would take Kristy away from her, so I gave her legal custody to remove her fear. Everything was fine in that respect.

My OCD symptoms continued to torture me. Most people didn't know about the stress I experienced with my compulsions. That's because I didn't tell anyone. People seemed to think I was being a clown when they saw me looking into space. And that's because I often did silly things. My silly behaviour was probably inconsistent with typical OCD behaviour, as it was somewhat impulsive. I will provide two examples of this in the following paragraphs.

I had a friend called Bray, who was a competitive long-distance runner. We went for runs together, and we sometimes did silly things. We enjoyed running in the rain and doing belly flops in puddles of water. One day we saw a storm coming, and we immediately put on our running shoes. But this storm developed into something extraordinary. The blackest cloud soon covered the entire city. Meanwhile, Bray and I ran up the road like roosters chosen for breeding. Suddenly, we were shocked by a white light and an explosion of thunder. We retreated to the nearest house like chicks to a mothering hen.

Bray and I drank alcohol one night per week, which occasionally led to trouble. On one occasion, Bray, myself, and a lad called Hynie went to a roadhouse to buy some food. I ordered a hamburger and a bucket of chips. The food came out quickly. Being hungry, intoxicated, and silly, I began eating the burger and the paper it was wrapped in. Suddenly an arm came over my shoulder and lifted me up by the head. My feet were off the floor and dangling. I was thrown on the floor, and a man began kicking me. I tried to get up from the floor while throwing uppercuts at the man's scrotum. Bray and I often used the word "scrotum" because it amused us. Anyway, the man clamped his legs together and blocked my uppercuts.

The violence continued. I was behind on points; Bray copped a punch to the lip; Hynie walked out of the toilet into a knuckle sandwich, and that was his feed for the night. Suddenly, the violence stopped. I heard Bray delivering a speech. I don't know what he said, but he seemed to capture everyone's attention. This was good because a group of bikers was beating us. All I remember about Bray's speech was his stupid ending. He said, "… now fuck off"! This stupid ending made the violence start again. The violence continued until someone said, "The cops are coming"! The bikies were gone within a couple of minutes. Apparently, the burger and chips belonged to one of the bikers.

About 10 months had passed since my last amateur fight. A friend had been offering to train me as a professional boxer. His name was John Cox. I decided to accept John's offer, and I had my first professional fight. My opponent was a former Australian champion who was past his prime.

Fight time arrived. My opponent and I fought up close a lot. My opponent would grunt when I hit him in the stomach. I thought I had found his weakness, so I continued to punch at his stomach (i.e., body punches). My opponent's blocking technique allowed some of my body punches to get through, and he continued to grunt when they got through. This made me try harder to land these body punches. It wasn't long before the body punches were no longer scoring cleanly. However, I continued to try hard to score with these punches.

I was fatigued when I reached the seventh round of this eight-round contest. My opponent finished strongly and won by a split decision. I learnt a lot about professional boxing in that fight, and this fellow was my teacher.

It was now eight months since my wife had left me. I then met a girl, and we started a relationship. This relationship didn't change my life much. That is, I continued to pursue my boxing career and do silly things.

My second professional fight was against a man called John Smith. John and I had sparred together as amateurs, and he was always better than me. This time we had a hard 10-round fight, which I won on points. I think John should have won the judge's decision, as my face was a mess.

My third fight was a rematch with John. I fought him differently this time. John usually moved around and touched me with jabs, and he'd uppercut me when I slipped under his jab. However, I didn't slip under his jab this time. I walked at him with my hands up and tried to bomb him with big punches. I did better this time. I knocked John down at the end of the fifth round, and I went back to my corner feeling confident.

John came out for the next round and attacked me. He usually didn't do that. His different approach surprised me. He cut both my eyelids in that round. The cuts bled into both eyes, and I don't think the referee knew it. My trainer tried to stop the bleeding between rounds, but John kept hitting the cuts. There were times when I was completely blind.

I became extremely tired as the fight continued. John hit me with a good punch on one of my cuts, and my will to fight drained out of me. John's trainer must have seen this. I heard him calling out: "He's yours; he's yours." These words weakened me even more. I looked to my corner and conveyed a message with my eyes (eyes that were intermittently blind). My message was: Do I have to do this? My trainer didn't recognise my distress.

I found the will to finish the fight, and the judges scored a draw. I believe the judges got it right. I won the first five rounds, and John won the last five. That was the hardest fight I ever had.

My next fight was a bad performance. I adjusted my defence to stop getting eye cuts, but it didn't work. I still received a bad cut over my eye. The referee said the cut was caused by an accidental head clash and the official result was a draw. The cut was really caused by a punch, but the referee didn't see it.

I then travelled to New South Wales for a fight. I tried very hard, but my performance was ordinary, and the judges scored against me. I drank alcohol after that fight. I got up in the morning with a bad hangover, a badly beaten body and sleep deprivation. But I still carried most of the luggage. I didn't have to carry all those bags. I did it because I was obsessed with pushing myself.

I then fought in Ipswich. I won that fight, and the Ipswich people celebrated. Ipswich people followed my progress, and I enjoyed the attention.

I did an extreme amount of physical training for boxing. I would run twice a day. I did boxing training every day (sometimes twice per day). I exercised with weights every day, which involved the same muscles each time. I never had a rest from training. I also held a full-time job. And I also suffered from extreme OCD symptoms, including insomnia.

With all this, my happiness continued to average 7.

Chapter 4

Finding a Life Outside Boxing

Age: 24 to 25

It was around this time that I became afflicted with headaches and fever. My poo went white, and my urine turned black. I went to the doctor, and a blood test confirmed hepatitis A. They didn't know much about hepatitis back then. I was told that I might experience relapses of this disease. That is, the disease might recur, and I might die from liver damage at an early age.

I was very worried about being sick for the rest of my life and dying early. I was also sad about not being able to box. My happiness went down to about 2. I had been depressed before, but this was different. I began to cry about things that weren't important. It felt like I was having a nervous breakdown. I don't know how much of this was due to toxins in my body, but I felt that I had to restore my mental health, or something inside me would break. The feeling in my nervous system really scared me; it made me stop worrying. In other words, the fear stopped me from worrying.

My girlfriend decided to break up with me around this time. This was probably due to the depressed mood I was suffering with at the time. I didn't want to break up with my girlfriend, but I was too proud to show a lot of emotion. I just left. I lived with Bray's parents then. I was still contagious with hepatitis, but Bray's parents allowed me to live with them. They were very kind to me.

Some time passed and I was no longer contagious. And my nervous system did get better. My liver was still in bad condition though. I had regular blood tests to monitor my liver. The doctor told me not to exercise while my liver was recovering. I really wanted to train for boxing, but I had to wait.

I met up with some people who were members of a church. I had previously attended this church, but I stopped attending because I couldn't understand its teaching. I told these people about my health problems and my breakup with my girlfriend. They heard my story and invited me to come to church again. I accepted their invitation, and I understood the teaching this time. It wasn't long before I was regularly attending church services.

I then decided to live with three young fellows who were competitive boxers. There was Paul (aged 17), John (aged 17), Jim (aged 14) and me (aged 24). These fellows were fun-loving guys, and they made me happy. Paul enjoyed jumping up and hitting his head on the ceiling. The broken ceiling represented the freedom we all shared. The four of us would go for trips in my car without knowing where we were going.

One day we were travelling towards the north coast, and we stopped to buy some pies. My intention was to walk away with the pie and then scream and throw my pie into the back of the pie van. I did that, and the man came out of his van and threw punches at Paul through the window. We drove away laughing ecstatically. We thought it was funny because Paul was being assaulted for something I had done.

One day the four of us went for a drive to Laidley. We had a big box of broken fruitcake with us on this occasion. We were driving down the range near Laidley and we passed a man who was changing a tyre on his car. The lads threw fruitcake at him. There was no icing on the fruitcake, so it wasn't a dangerous act. Anyway, the man finished changing his tyre, chased us down the range, and rammed into our car. He was obviously having a bad day, and we made it worse.

We continued down the range and headed towards Laidley. We drove through the main street and approached the railway crossing. We could see a group of people in a shed near the railway crossing. We stopped and asked these people for some information. We were really looking for entertainment. One of the men spoke to us. He said that they were having a meeting, and we disturbed them. We thought he was rude, so we threw fruitcake at all of them. These people became angry and chased us. We didn't want to hurt anyone, so we jumped in the car and proceeded to drive away.

A train stopped us from crossing the railway track, so we turned around and drove up the road beside the railway track. We crossed the overhead bridge and travelled back along the other side of the railway track. Meanwhile, these people had crossed the pedestrian bridge and joined hands to form a human chain across the road. They were daring me to run over them. This was a test involving mental stress. My experience with OCD had conditioned me for mental stress, so their trick was never going to work. They moved aside as I drove through slowly.

Why did I carry out the above-mentioned behaviours? As this book is chronological, I will answer this question with the limited knowledge I possessed at that time. That is, I was extremely active (both physically and mentally). And being crazy was normal for me. I wasn't boxing at the time because my liver was still recovering. Not having an activity made me even more crazy. And the other boys were just young and cheeky.

My OCD symptoms continued to torture me. I also continued to attend church services. I was becoming more serious about my faith.

I then met a girl called Marlene, whom I called Polly. A relationship developed between us, and the young fellows moved out of the house. I had lived with them for one year, and my happiness averaged **7** during that time.

Chapter 5

I Felt Physically Insurmountable

Age: 25 to 26

I had regular blood tests to monitor the recovery of my liver. My liver improved when I didn't exercise and became worse when I did. I wanted to resume boxing, but I had to be patient.

I thought about my boxing technique while my liver was recovering. I discovered a better technique. I also read books about the science of exercise and realised that I had overtrained throughout my entire boxing career. I was keen to resume boxing and apply my new technique and my new exercise program.

Time passed. It was now nine months since I initially contracted hepatitis. My liver had recovered, and I began training again. I started with an easy routine, but I was soon overtraining again. It was hard to stop myself from overtraining. However, I did manage to reduce my running. I won my first fight and then kept on winning. I had six fights in seven months and won them all. The duration of my fights was 10 rounds, and I beat my opponents because they became tired in the later rounds. I had reduced my running, and I was now performing at a higher level.

Although I was performing well in my fights, my

OCD symptoms were extremely stressful. With this, my happiness remained at **7**. It may seem strange to rate my happiness so highly when my OCD was so stressful. However, this "happiness rating" is not a measurement of my stress; it is a measurement of my happiness (i.e., moods).

My next fight was supposed to be a big test for me. John (my trainer) must have thought this fight needed special training. He advised me to take two weeks off work and to do some sparring at Reg Layton's gym. I sparred at Reg's gym in the morning and boxed with John in the afternoon. This was extra boxing training. However, I decided to stop my weight training for those two weeks.

I had my final sparring session four days before the fight. I weighed myself after that sparring session, and I was three kilograms under the middleweight limit. I was advised to stop training, so I did.

The weigh-in was held on the day before the fight. I stepped onto the scales and discovered that I had gained one-and-a-half kilograms in three days. This was not fluid weight; it was real body weight. I had never gained this kind of weight before a fight. However, I had never stopped training four days before a fight.

Fight time arrived. The bell rang to start the first round. My opponent punched very hard. I knew I had to fight him at close range because he had a long reach. Fortunately, I was able to slip under his punches. Round two started. I was having success with my right uppercut when we fought at close range. I really lifted the uppercut because he was easy to hit with that punch. I hit him on the forehead with an uppercut and broke my hand. I knew my hand was broken, but I kept using it. I kept using it because I was insanely determined. My hand hurt in round three and round four, and then it went numb.

It was now round five. My opponent hit me with two consecutive hooks on both sides of my chin. I lost my sense of hearing, and my vision was almost gone, but my cognitive awareness remained. I was aware that my eyes would appear dazed. And I knew my opponent would see my dazed eyes and attack me. And I knew I had to disguise my eyes to stop him from attacking me. I made my vacant eyes look angry, and my opponent did not attack me. I managed to recover.

The fight continued. My opponent had more power than me, but he seemed inexperienced. I was able to block his body punches like my opponent blocked mine in my first professional fight. He became fatigued in the later rounds, and I won the fight. I was now the number one contender for the Australian title.

The interesting thing about the above story is that my cognitive awareness remained when I was almost unconscious. It seemed like my thoughts were so forceful that they could pervade semi-consciousness. Another example is, I could be resting and almost asleep, and if I had to get up for some reason – I would experience a kind of power that would raise me up. This was a burden because I could not be gentle to myself.

I sustained a lot of injuries in the above-mentioned fight. I had a torn rib cartilage, a cut on top of my head, a massive hole in my eyebrow, and a broken hand. I had to take time off boxing while my injuries were healing. During this time, I began to think about my compulsions and how they affected me during my fights. I'd hold on to my opponents and check my thoughts when I fought up close. I'd move away from my opponents and check my thoughts when I fought at a long distance. The compulsions were very dangerous when I fought at a distance because my opponent could hit me. My attention was not on my opponent when I was compulsively checking my thoughts. I only had a few seconds to snap out of the compulsion, and those few seconds were terrifying.

Chapter 6

The Church, Polly, Family and Leaving the Railways

Age: 26 to 34

Marlene (Polly) and I were spending a lot of time together, and I asked her to marry me. She said yes. We had the wedding ceremony at Polly's house and the reception in a little croquet hall. Relatives and friends were invited to the reception. The railway boys occupied the clowns' table, and I put my face in the wedding cake. Everyone had a great time.

My life changed then. It didn't change because I was married. It changed because I wasn't training for fights anymore. I was still waiting for my injuries to heal. I continued to think about my compulsions and the risks involved with boxing. These thoughts were influenced by my obsessive view of the church's teaching. That is, I was afraid of not fulfilling my responsibility to God. Furthermore, Polly and I had started a family, and I was afraid of becoming a brain-damaged father. I decided to retire from boxing and devote my life to church and family.

My time was now spent working in the railway workshops, playing with the children, and attending church activities. Our life was busy but well-balanced.

Polly and I had very different personalities. Polly was

good at things that I wasn't. I was good at understanding deep and meaningful things, but Polly was not. She was good at spelling and remembering the names of things, but I was not. We also dealt with life's challenges in a different way. For example, I confronted stressful thoughts, but Polly ignored them. We struggled with our different personalities, but something always enabled us to work through it.

Seven years passed. Polly and I had three children. Jason was born first. Tim was born three years later, and Andy was born four years after Tim. My life didn't change much during those seven years. My happiness averaged about **6** during that time.

I was now 33 years old. I had been suffering from compulsions for 16 years, and I had never consulted a psychiatrist. I then decided to do that. The psychiatrist diagnosed me with OCD. (Refer Appendix A at the end of this book for signs and symptoms of OCD.)

The psychiatrist prescribed a drug called Anafranil, which made me tired. I stopped taking this drug after one week. The psychiatrist then prescribed a drug called Prozac, which also made me tired. I stopped taking that drug too. I didn't want to be tired.

My compulsions involved anxiety that provoked intense thinking. It was extremely difficult to resist these compulsions. One day I decided to do something I had not done before. I decided to completely resist a compulsion. I was shopping for groceries at the time. My anxiety pulsated for 10 seconds as I refused to carry out the intense thinking (compulsion). I then found myself racing madly down the aisle. I was looking for something. I stopped and wondered what I was looking for. I didn't know. I then realised that my anxiety had ceased, and I had burst into a hyperactive frenzy. This experience allowed me to understand that mental energy was fuelling my anxiety, my intense thinking, and my hyperactivity. I could also *feel* that this mental energy could make me have Tourette's tics. The experience in the grocery shop enabled me to extrapolate that my OCD, and my undiagnosed ADHD and Tourette Syndrome (TS) were associated through excessive mental energy (high arousal).

I mentioned my arousal theory to the psychiatrist. He said my theory was very interesting, but it would be hard to prove. It was now 1992. At this time, behavioural science had known that OCD and TS were associated because these disorders were observed in family units. They didn't seem to know any more than that.

Chapter 7

Studying

Age: 34 to 38

Another year passed. The Ipswich Railway Workshops were now reducing staff. They offered me a redundancy package of $38,000, which included my long service payment. I accepted this money and left the railways. I had worked there for 18 years.

I tried to hold boilermaking jobs when I left the railways, but I didn't have enough skill. I tried labouring jobs, but I couldn't hold onto those either. I tried very hard, but I couldn't do the work fast enough.

I then enrolled in a pre-apprenticeship course in fitting and turning. I thought this would improve my trade skills. However, I couldn't keep up with the other students. I was a qualified tradesman, and I couldn't keep up with a class of inexperienced boys. I then realised how much Queensland Rail had supported me for 18 years.

One day I was discussing my situation with a Centrelink officer. I disclosed my failure to complete the fitting and turning course, and my basic inability to perform. I began to cry while I was talking to the Centrelink officer. The officer seemed to believe that I was suffering from ADHD, and he advised me to see a doctor.

I consulted a doctor, who referred me to a psychiatrist. I consulted a psychiatrist, who referred me to the public hospital for a series of psychological tests. The psychiatrist said that the waiting time for these hospital appointments could be quite long.

Meanwhile, I wanted to do something with my life. I wanted to earn a living. I thought about working in the fitness industry, as I was always interested in physical fitness. I needed to complete a fitness leadership course to do this. Although my childhood experience with school predicted failure, I thought my knowledge about fitness would make the course easier. Furthermore, my compulsions were improving. Therefore, I decided to enrol in the course.

My knowledge of fitness did make the course easier. However, I still needed to work hard. I worked very hard.

I discovered that administrative duties were involved in the fitness industry. I thought these administrative duties would be too hard for me, so I finished the course and didn't pursue the fitness industry.

I really wanted to have an occupation. I was 34 years old, and I hadn't found anything I was good at. However, my experience with the fitness leader's course made me realise that mature-aged students were well-supported. This made me wonder if I could find a suitable job by studying.

I looked at my options and decided to enrol in adult tertiary preparation (ATP). The ATP course was equal to year 12 at school. It was a TAFE-level course. People who enrolled in ATP were required to do a pre-course test, which would predict their ability to do the course. I received a low score on this test because I didn't have enough time. The course counsellor thought I wouldn't cope with full-time study, and she advised me to enrol in part-time study. However, I needed to do full-time study to receive Austudy payments. Austudy payments would allow me to study without having to work.

I spoke to Polly about the idea of studying full-time, and we agreed that I had nothing to lose by trying. Therefore, I enrolled in the ATP course as a full-time student. Full-time students had to choose a minimum of four subjects. I chose a subject that contained the same content as the fitness leader's course, which would reduce my workload.

I started the ATP course at the beginning of the following year. It turned out that many circumstances helped me to study. The reduced workload helped me. Polly's support helped me. The teachers were very dedicated. I received personal tutoring for spelling. I utilised all this help and worked long hours. The duration of the course was one year, and I graduated with one honour, two credits, and a pass (for four subjects). My happiness averaged 7 during that year. My happiness had improved because I liked what I was doing. My OCD symptoms also continued to improve.

I was now ready for tertiary studies. Well, that's what they told me. I looked at the courses that were available. Many of the courses required a higher OP score than I had. (An OP score was relative to a person's previous achievement, which was my ATP results.)

There was one course called human and community services, which didn't require a high OP score. This course provided skills to work in community welfare, which involved helping people. It was a TAFE-level course, so it would be easier than university studies. I thought this course was perfect for me, so I enrolled.

I started the welfare course at the beginning of the new year. Therefore, my full-time studies continued, and my Austudy payments also continued. The welfare course involved a lot of group interaction, which gave me the opportunity to ask questions about things I missed in class (due to my poor concentration). Many circumstances continued to help me to study.

I then received a call from the public hospital regarding the series of psychological tests, which the psychiatrist had previously ordered. This led to a diagnosis of ADHD accompanied with Tourette Syndrome. (Refer Appendix B for signs and symptoms of ADHD, and Appendix C for signs and symptoms of Tourette Syndrome.)

After receiving the above diagnosis, my psychiatrist prescribed a psycho-stimulant drug called Dexamphetamine. This drug was supposed to help me concentrate. I took the drug, and it helped me to persevere with my studies. However, my concentration was still poor.

The welfare course provided an opportunity to compare my concentration with other students. I compared my concentration during reading activities (in class). That is, the teacher would ask us to read something, and we would then discuss what we had read. She would begin the discussion when most of the class were finished reading. I was often a little more than one quarter through the passage when most of the class were finished reading. Therefore, I frequently observed myself to read three-and-a-half times slower than the average TAFE student. This was only a test for reading speed, but other activities were affected in the same way as my reading. It was definitely a concentration problem.

My observation in the classroom was important because I could now quantify my concentration problem (i.e., three to four times slower than average). This gave me a more accurate understanding of how my brain was working.

By now, my OCD had been improving for three

years. My compulsions had greatly reduced. I reduced them by defying fear. I reduced my fear by doing what I wanted to do (regardless of fear). I was then confronted with another opportunity to defy fear. I will explain this in the paragraph below.

I began to experience the desire to box again. The idea of returning to boxing scared me in two ways. I was afraid of neglecting my responsibility to God, and becoming a brain-damaged father. However, I was inspired to surpass these fears. Therefore, I made a commitment to box again. I was offered a fight, and I accepted.

The day of the fight arrived. The weigh-in was held in the morning, and the fights were in the afternoon. I was heavier than my opponent, so I sat in a hot bath to sweat some weight off. We then travelled to the Gold Coast for the weigh-in. I weighed in and then went to the beach with Polly. We spent a couple of hours in the sun and then went to the venue to get ready for the fight. I arrived at the venue and discovered the fights were being held outside (in the sun).

Fight time arrived. I went out to the ring and was surprised by the glaring sun. And we fought hard in the sun. My body became extremely weak in the fifth round. I had one-and-a-half rounds to go. I managed to finish the fight and win by a split points decision. I had a terrible headache after that fight, which lasted for three days.

I stopped boxing after that. I continued to devote myself to the church, my family, and the welfare course. The welfare course taught us about social institutions, politics, various cultures, and business. The course provider and the teachers were great. I was a very enthusiastic student. I was driven by the desire to find my niche and earn a living. The course took one year to complete, and I eventually passed all my subjects. My happiness continued to average **7**.

Completing the welfare course gave me a higher OP score, which would allow me to study psychology at the University of Southern Queensland (USQ). I doubted my ability to succeed in a university-level course, but I decided to look into it anyway. I found that students with disabilities were allowed concessions at USQ. I was also eligible for concessions through Austudy. I was eligible for these concessions because I was officially diagnosed with ADHD and TS. There were many concessions, and they were very generous: USQ would extend the duration of the course from three to six years; Austudy would extend my payments for the whole six years; USQ would give me extra time to complete exams. The concessions were almost unbelievable. But the deal got even better.

The course had two modes of study (internal mode and external mode). Students studying the internal mode would attend lectures on campus. Students studying in the external mode would have learning material sent to their homes. The external mode would be self-paced because I could decide when I wanted to study. This meant that I could work long hours. The concessions were very generous, and the conditions were perfect. Polly and I agreed that I had nothing to lose by trying. Therefore, I enrolled in the external mode of the psychology course through USQ.

I started the psychology course at the beginning of the year. Therefore, my full-time studies just continued. I was very interested in the material I was learning. However, I read no wider than the learning objectives because I needed to manage my time. I recorded the information regarding these learning objectives on audio tapes. I could then prepare for exams by listening to the tapes. This reduced my reading, which was good because I was very slow at reading.

I also met a lady who helped me a lot. She proofread

my essays and coached me with academic writing. Polly gave me great support while I was studying, and USQ also gave me great support. I utilised all this support and worked consistently and efficiently.

We were sometimes given a choice of topics to write essays on. I chose to write an essay on the difference between Buddhism and Hinduism. I stayed up all night researching this topic. I always knew when the sun was coming up because I'd hear the birds tweeting. That was my sign to go to bed. I'd have two hours sleep and wake up to find that my writing was disjointed. I almost gave up on this essay because it was taking so much time. Miraculously, my writing suddenly came together. I didn't have this problem again. So, what caused this problem? Well, I was heavily involved in my church, and my mind was burdened by what I perceived as conflicting views. Having to work through these conflicting views was a significant part of the problem.

I continued to divide my time between church, family, and my studies. I got into the habit of sleeping five nights per week, and I used my time efficiently. My happiness continued to average 7.

Chapter 8

A Clear Path

Age: 38 to 40

I was now in my second year of the psychology course. I was very interested in psychology. I was particularly interested in OCD, ADHD and TS. I had a theory that OCD, ADHD and TS were associated through arousal. I established this theory five years ago, and I wrote about it in chapter six. However, I encountered something that prompted me to add to this theory. I will copy part of chapter six so that my theory can be revised. I will then explain how I added to it.

> *From Chapter 6: "My compulsions involved anxiety that provoked intense thinking. It was extremely difficult to resist these compulsions. One day, I decided to do something I had not done before: I decided to completely resist a compulsion. I was shopping for groceries at the time. My anxiety pulsated for ten seconds as I refused to carry out the compulsion (intense thinking). I then found myself racing madly down the aisle. I was looking for something. I stopped and wondered what I was looking for. I didn't know. I then realised that my anxiety had ceased, and I had burst into a hyperactive*

frenzy. This experience allowed me to understand that mental energy was fuelling my anxiety, my intense thinking, and my hyperactivity. I could also feel that this mental energy could make me have Tourette's tics. This experience enabled me to extrapolate that my OCD, and my undiagnosed ADHD and Tourette Syndrome (TS) were associated through excessive mental energy (high arousal).

I want to make sure you understand what I mean by arousal before I explain how I added to my theory. The arousal I am referring to is not a temporary and fluctuating state. Rather, it's more like a person's nature. I sometimes call it 'mental energy' (as you can see above). Both terms mean the same thing.

How I added to my theory:

My old theory was limited to the idea that high arousal was fuelling the anxiety of my OCD, the hyperactivity and attention deficit of my ADHD, and the explosive hyperactivity of my TS symptoms. My extended theory included an additional way arousal affected my OCD. You see, high arousal was bleeping out my concentration. My thoughts would substantially disappear from my working memory. I was catapulted to a conclusion, and I didn't know how I got there. That made me anxious about my conclusion. High arousal then fuelled this anxiety and made it intense. Anxiety (being intensified) would then drive me to rethink, because I wanted to be sure about my conclusion. I would rethink again but I still couldn't remember my thoughts because they had disappeared from my memory again. I would rethink again and again and again. These repetitive thoughts were extremely intense because I'd strain to remember them. It was an attention deficit that made my thoughts disappear from my working memory. This attention deficit/concentration problem is a symptom of ADHD, but it was also a part of my OCD symptoms. It was an additional link between my ADHD and OCD. THIS was the addition to my theory.

My extended theory gave me a greater understanding of how excessive arousal affected me. It was the primary cause of my compulsions, hyperactivity, and TS symptoms—and the complete cause of my concentration problem (second-by-second).

I believe people who are diagnosed with only one of these three disorders may have high arousal, or they may not. I will explain why.

The following three paragraphs may require knowledge about behavioural science.

1. **Regarding OCD:** People may have symptoms of OCD, but they may be partly inclined towards obsessive-compulsive personality disorder (OCPD). And high arousal is not likely to be the primary cause of OCPD because the personality is the primary cause. Also, some people with OCD may be more affected by phobias. Attention deficit part of OCD may not be involved in this. In other words, they may have conditioned fears and not high arousal.

2. **Regarding ADHD:** There are three basic symptoms of ADHD: inattention, hyperactivity and impulsivity (Refer Appendix B for signs and symptoms of ADHD. Some people diagnosed with ADHD can have difficulty maintaining their attention on a task that doesn't interest them. This is especially true with dual diagnoses. However, a person with a second-by-second attention problem will have trouble with any task that involves a working memory. Being

interested in it won't help. Even self-determination doesn't help. Psychological tests can prove this. Another symptom of ADHD is hyperactivity. However, people without high arousal may *appear* hyperactive because they do *not* use their arousal (mental energy) to think about things. Therefore, their arousal is used to carry out physical behaviours that can be seen. The other symptom is impulsivity. Impulsivity can be increased through selective perception. In summary, without an appropriate test for high arousal, it is hard to know what is causing the symptoms of ADHD.

3. **Regarding TS:** I believe TS symptoms are a strong predictor of high arousal. However, it is known that extreme stress can cause TS symptoms. These symptoms may go away when the stress subsides. It seems reasonable to me that extreme stress could hype up all these disorders.

The above three paragraphs explain how symptoms of these disorders can have various causes. I believe people with only one of these disorders have less chance of having high arousal. This is because another cause will most likely give rise to only one of these disorders. People with two of these three disorders would have a much greater chance of having high arousal. People with all three disorders would *certainly* have high arousal. In other words, the probability of having high arousal increases with the number of disorders because high arousal is the link.

I will continue with my life story now.

There were two paths that existed for me. There was the conservative path and the path of freedom. The conservative path was the OCD path, which trapped me in the stressful habit of checking my thoughts. I chose to be free from that stress, so I chose the path of freedom. And I progressed on this path through overcoming fear. And I overcame fear through doing what I wanted to do (regardless of fear). I had been progressing on this path of freedom for the last seven years.

My addition to my theory (mentioned above) enabled me to understand this path of freedom more clearly. This clearer understanding motivated me to live even more freely. This is how I eradicated the deeper roots of my OCD.

Chapter 9

Back to Boxing and then Rejections

Age: 40 to 46

I was now three-and-a-half years into the psychology course. The grades for these university subjects were: fail, pass, credit, distinction, and high distinction. I was achieving credits for my subjects. Polly continued to support me in every way. I had been sleeping five nights per week since I started the course, and I utilised this time for my faith, my family, and my studies.

My strong mental energy made me seek a busy lifestyle. This produced the urge to box again. However, I had certain fears about this. I was afraid of neglecting my faith and family. I experienced mental warfare when I processed the urge to box. But I recognised my fear, and I thought fear was negative. Eventually, I did what I wanted to do (regardless of fear). I took up boxing again.

I won my first two fights. Then, my knowledge of physical training became smothered by obsessive delusion. I began overtraining and dieting too much. I'd finish studying at 3.00 am and go for a run. Sometimes I'd run 35 km without drinking fluid. Sometimes I did my boxing training with heavy plastic clothes on.

My third comeback fight was for the state welterweight title. The welterweight limit was 66.5 kg, which was six kilograms lighter than when I fought in my twenties. I had broken two ribs prior to this title fight, and they hadn't healed properly. I also didn't think my blood pressure was right because I often felt dizzy.

Fight time arrived. I did okay in the first round, but my opponent re-broke one of my ribs in the second round. I quit at the end of the fourth round. My decision to quit was a guess because I wasn't sure how I felt. It was hard to know how I felt because my determination seemed unlimited. I had a fuzzy perception of physical limitation. I had this when I was a child, and it never went away.

I was then asked to fight a Ukrainian boxer. This fellow was an excellent amateur who was having his first professional fight. He'd won numerous amateur titles, and he was four kilograms heavier than me. I knew I'd be outclassed. However, I really wanted to have a fight. I accepted the fight, but I wasn't happy with the matchup.

My unhappiness with the matchup caused me to make a foolish decision. That is, I decided I would quit if I was outclassed. Boxers tend to make bad decisions when they manage themselves. I was self-managed and self-trained.

Fight time arrived. My opponent was a lot taller than me. He kept touching me with a jab and moving away. I didn't score a single punch in the first round. The second round started, and the same thing happened again. I was being outclassed. As planned, I pretended to be hurt, and the fight was stopped.

I was eventually offered a rematch with the fellow I had fought for the state welterweight title. My back was sore in this fight because I had been training with broken ribs. I was taking anti-inflammatory medication for the pain. I suffered a bad cut above my eyebrow in this fight. Blood was pulsating out of my eyebrow, and the referee stopped the fight. I was glad the referee stopped the fight because I was tired. I was tired because I was fighting below my natural weight.

I was now in the fifth year of my psychology course. I had continued to miss two nights' sleep per week. I was also doing too much exercise and taking a lot of head punches. Strangely, I continued to achieve credits for my subjects, and my happiness remained at **7**.

I had another fight and won on points. I was then matched with a strong young fellow. I saw this fellow walking around before we fought. Someone called out to him, and his head appeared to turn 180 degrees (like a parrot). This affected my confidence. Anyway, the fight started. The man with the extra rotating head had too much endurance for me. I quit with two rounds remaining in the fight. I felt guilty for quitting during that fight. I didn't feel guilty for quitting against the Ukrainian boxer, or in the welterweight title fight. However, I could not justify quitting in this fight. So why did I quit? I thought deeply about this question, and my answer is provided below.

I still had a fuzzy perception of physical limitation. That is, I had an insane ability to push my body. I was 42 years old and fighting superior opponents. I knew boxing was a dangerous sport. And it would be extra dangerous to push my body according to my ability to do so. The situation was even more complicated because I had a good chin. In other words, it was hard to knock me out. Therefore, I would continue to take dangerous punches as the fight went on. And being afraid of becoming a brain-damaged father lay beneath the whole problem. But what was I going to do about the problem? I also thought deeply about this question.

Again, I concluded that the problem was fear. And the solution was to deal with the fear. I had been dealing with fear by doing what I wanted to do. This was how I eliminated the mental platform from which compulsions arose. It was my path to freedom. And this was just another obstacle on this path. Therefore, I simply decided not to quit anymore.

I was still attending church services three times a week. The church had served my needs for many years, but some things were concerning me now. I was concerned that I was caring too much about my faith. I believed this caused fear—which wasn't a Godly thing. Furthermore, reducing fear was a factor of my path. Therefore, I began to reduce my obsessive devotion to my faith.

I was now in the final year of my psychology course. It was during this year that I studied counselling psychology. Counselling psychology was a subject where students had a choice of assignments they could do. I chose to do an assignment on existentialism. I defined existentialism as: A philosophy concerned with finding who and what we are without the influence of collective ideas or traditions.

Existential philosophy appealed to me because it strengthened my belief in doing what I wanted to do. It strengthened my motivation to defy fear. I was already free from compulsions that tortured me, but I wanted to be freer than that. I wanted to freely express my mental energy. Only then could I fully understand myself. Therefore, the assignment on existentialism helped me to proceed further on this path, which I had been on for the last nine years.

Counselling psychology required the most creativity out of all the subjects in the course. I achieved a high distinction for that subject. It was the only high distinction I achieved during the entire course.

I was now finished my psychology degree. It took me exactly six years to complete the course, which was the maximum time I was allowed with my concessions. I learnt wonderful things during that course.

I had now completed three courses in eight years. I had great support from Polly, Centrelink, and all the education providers. I utilised all that support and studied consistently. My happiness averaged 7 during those eight years (with minimal fluctuation).

I was now looking forward to starting work. I couldn't practise psychology because I only completed an undergraduate degree. I needed to complete postgraduate studies to practise psychology. My writing coach believed that postgraduate studies would be too hard for me. I always took her advice.

I was keen to find a job as a welfare worker. I applied for jobs but had no success. I decided to gain some practical experience through volunteer work. I found a volunteer position. The volunteers' role was to provide emotional support to members of troubled families. The volunteers had to complete a short course. Successful volunteers were selected according to their performance in the course. I began the course by explaining my concentration problem to the course facilitator, whose name was Jane Smith. Jane was willing to cater for my needs.

The course involved a lot of class interaction and not much reading. Once again, I had found a course that suited me. Part of our training involved roleplays. The roleplays were designed to make us aware of sensitive issues that might affect our work with clients. We were placed in pairs for these roleplays. Our partner would play the role of a person who had hurt our feelings, which could be a sensitive issue.

Firstly, we had to think of someone who our partner could be. I had a problem with that. I couldn't think of anyone who my partner could be. There was nobody in the world that I had a problem with. I was continuously urged to think of someone, but I couldn't. I didn't have any sensitive issues that I could think of. Most of the participants had asked their partner to play the role of their father or mother. I had forgiven my parents for any wrong they had done to me. And I had forgiven everyone else. Nothing seemed to be troubling me in that way. However, I selected one of my parents (just to cooperate).

The roleplays commenced. My partner did her best to play the role of my parent. I also did my best to play the role of myself. However, I couldn't meet the demands of the roleplay. That is, I couldn't express my problem to my partner (my parent) because I didn't have one. My partner expressed her frustration to the course facilitator. "It doesn't worry him. He doesn't care," she said. The fact was, I didn't have any issues with anyone from my past. It seemed to be unusual to not have a problem like this. But that's how it was.

As I mentioned, the volunteers were being trained to provide emotional support to members of troubled families. We were trained to do this through showing empathy. Our ability to show empathy was assessed throughout the course. Successful volunteers were selected at the end of the course. I was selected.

It was now six months since I'd finished studying, and I still hadn't found a paying job. I then heard that volunteers were needed to support mentally ill people within a hospital setting. The volunteers' role was to accompany patients during their activities and just talk with them. I had to complete a short induction course before I could start. Again, the course did not involve much reading, and I was able to qualify. I then worked within the criminally insane section of the hospital.

My first experience with supporting criminally insane

patients was playing volleyball with them. I found that most of these patients suffered from schizophrenia and bipolar disorder. Sufferers of these disorders often experience hallucinations. I had met people with these disorders when I was working with the church. It was interesting to talk with them. They seemed to be dreaming when they were awake. That is, they seemed to experience an abnormal state of consciousness. However, that's just my view.

Meanwhile, I continued to box. I no longer had OCD symptoms during fights, but I had TS symptoms instead. I would intensely squeeze my eyes closed during fights. I'd hold on to my opponent and squeeze my eyes closed when I fought in close. I also squeezed my eyes closed when I fought at a distance. I would move away and do it. This was scary because I knew my opponent might come forward and hit me. I only had a few seconds to stop doing it. I had a similar experience when I was in my twenties, but it was OCD symptoms. I now had TS symptoms instead of OCD symptoms. My accumulated knowledge enabled me to understand why this was so. It was the same arousal, which was fuelling TS symptoms instead of OCD symptoms.

By now, my obsessive devotion to my faith had reduced. I had begun to confront questions regarding my church's beliefs. This was a serious situation because I had given my life to this church. I attended three church services and one seminar per week, and I was involved with Sunday school, family visiting, and mission work. I had done this for 18 years, but now, I was questioning it all. I had come to the point where I had to decide if I should stay in the church or leave it. This was a scary decision to make. I'd been on a path of freedom for 10 years now, and this decision seemed to be another obstacle in the way.

I didn't suffer from compulsions anymore, but the decision to leave the church or remain in it caused compulsive thoughts to come back (only regarding this situation). I spent many sleepless nights labouring through compulsive thoughts. I counted the reasons why I should continue in the church and why I should not. I'd miscount the reasons, and then I'd count them again, and again, and again. Early one morning, in a bed soaked with perspiration, I decided to leave the church.

Leaving the church left an enormous void in my life. I had much less to do and much less to think about. Finishing my studies also left an enormous void. The combination of these two situations changed my life enormously in a very short time. I experienced extreme boredom and uncertainty, and my mind was seriously affected.

I eventually gained a paid position as a family service officer. I was responsible for the case management of young people on court orders. I was to occupy this position for 11 weeks while someone was on leave. I thought this job might lead to a permanent job. I stopped my volunteer work with criminally insane patients while I occupied this position. My boredom and uncertainty improved through this opportunity. And my happiness improved.

The new job required a lot of rote learning. I was very slow at rote learning. I worked 12 hours of overtime per week without being paid for it. I didn't tell anyone because I didn't want anyone to know about my slowness. The 11-week term was soon finished. I wanted a good report from my supervisor, as this would help me get a more suitable job. I didn't get the report I wanted, and that made me sad.

I was offered a youth worker position in the same department. However, my poor concentration affected me in that job too. I lost the youth worker job, and that made me sad again.

I was now finished with the abovementioned department. I enquired about resuming my volunteer work with criminally insane patients. The boss told me to repeat the course. I believed this man didn't like me, and I had an argument with him on the phone. I was easily prompted to anger by now. I was losing hope, and I was becoming self-destructive.

I was still doing volunteer work with troubled families. I was only doing this for a couple of hours per week. However, things began to change in that department. Jane (the coordinator) left the organisation. Her replacement worker was a kind and genuine person like Jane. But she only stayed a little while, and then left. There was another worker within the organisation who I admired. She also left. These ladies understood my disability and trusted me. Now they were gone. I was very frustrated. Someone within the organisation saw me expressing my frustration. As a result, I lost that position. And this added to my frustration. I was becoming increasingly sad and angry. I was becoming self-destructive.

I had begun to smoke marijuana. I only smoked five or six cones per week. Smoking marijuana made me susceptible to compulsions, but I resisted the compulsions when I smoked it. This made me less susceptible to compulsions when I didn't smoke it. Therefore, smoking marijuana probably helped me to remove my deepest OCD inclinations. I don't recommend that OCD sufferers smoke marijuana because it might have a different effect on them.

Inactivity made me extremely bored. Overcoming the deeper roots of OCD increased my boredom because I didn't think as much. I was losing hope of finding a suitable job and I was becoming angrier.

I was still boxing, but the Australian National Boxing Federation (ANBF) was saying that I shouldn't be allowed to box. They said I was too old, and I was losing too many fights. I was losing because I was accepting fights with superior boxers. However, I wasn't being knocked out or knocked down, and I was passing my pre-fight medicals. Anyway, the ANBF had a meeting and decided to allow me to continue boxing, but they were watching me.

I then fought another strong young fellow. I was going okay in this fight, but I kept slipping on the signage that was on the floor. The slippery floor really affected me in the last round. This fellow hit me with his right hand and broke my nose. He then hit me with another right hand and wrecked my nose even more. Then a third right hand hit me in the same place, and I was sniffing around corners. The referee stopped the contest.

The ANBF was now more serious about revoking my boxing licence. I started refusing fights with strong opponents because the ANBF was on my case. My boxing activity then slowed down.

I now had very little to do. I was a hyperactive person, and I needed to be busy. I spent most of my days alone because I didn't have friends. My boredom was bad, and my anger was getting worse.

I did have one friend. I will call him "Old Mate". Old Mate was a hyperactive fellow like me. We went on journeys in my car and did clowning activities. We called these clowning activities "serving", and we called ourselves "The Community Servants"—and we called my car "The Servant". These clowning activities reduced the pain of my boredom. It really wasn't enough, but it's all I had.

I eventually received an offer to have a fight. My son (Jason) was asked to fight on the same program. I accepted this offer because I didn't think my opponent would hurt me too much. Jason won his fight, but I lost mine due to a cut-eye ruling. I bled all over the place. I was now sure the ANBF would revoke my licence, so I retired to stop them from doing it. I had 30 fights between the ages of 40 and 46. I enjoyed the boxing activity because it gave me a challenge. But my boxing was now finished.

I tried to contact Old Mate, but I couldn't. I think he went overseas. I felt like I had nothing to live for. I was bored, lonely, and angry. People didn't validate my reason for being angry. They couldn't understand that a person could have such limited opportunities to do things. They couldn't understand that most activities didn't interest me because they weren't intense enough. They couldn't understand that poor concentration limited my opportunities. They couldn't understand that inactivity was extra painful for a hyperactive person. And I didn't have friends. I guess they couldn't understand because my situation was unusual.

I couldn't see any way to help myself. I was in a mental tangle, and I pulled angrily at the threads. Sometimes I'd explode. I'd walk in the direction of oncoming cars and force them off the road. I'd have fits of rage. I'd scream, smash things, and bash my head on things until I became exhausted, and I'd fall to the ground and cry. I'd cry for two minutes and then get up and do the same thing again. One day of anger was followed by one day of depression. This happened twice per week. I had four days of hell every week. And this cycle continued for six months.

My happiness averaged **1.5** during that six-months.

Chapter 10

I Found My Niche

Age: 46 to 47

I had recently grown two marijuana plants at home. The plants were very small because I had grown them in small pots. I decided to grow more of these plants. I had some seeds, and I went searching for a place to plant them. I had recently taken the drug LSD, which I usually didn't do.

I wanted to plant these marijuana seeds amongst lantana bushes. Lantana is a prickly weed that will sometimes grow taller than an adult human. I was moving through tall lantana in an unfamiliar place, and I wasn't aware that the sun was going down. Suddenly, it became quite dark, and I couldn't find a way out of this snake-infested place. Suddenly, I saw a spinning yellow light hovering above the lantana, and I heard voices coming from it. It was illegal to be in this place, and I thought the authorities were chasing me. I thought they were chasing me in a monster truck with a yellow light on top. I started running away from this yellow light.

I stumbled over ditches and fell into holes, as I ran from the yellow spinning light. The prickly lantana wrapped around me and cut my skin. Eventually, the prickly lantana stopped me from running, and I crawled along the ground. I don't remember how long I crawled, but I do remember getting back on my feet and walking. The machine with the yellow spinning light must have gone away because it was gone from my mind. I continued to push through the lantana, but I couldn't find a way out.

I eventually got out of the lantana. It was now nighttime, and I had no idea where I was. I decided to walk in one direction because I knew this strategy would lead me somewhere. I eventually found a railway line. I walked along this railway line for 20 minutes until it went in two directions. One line went to the twinkling lights of suburbia, and the other line went to the right. I looked towards the twinkling lights, and I looked to the right. I then saw my car. The Servant was shining in the moonlight.

I learnt later that the yellow spinning light was on an earth-moving machine, which was operating about half a kilometre from where I was.

I eventually found places to cultivate my marijuana seeds. It was hard to till the soil in this area because there was a lot of clay, and the clay was dry and hard. Experienced marijuana growers would not select such places, but I was a novice. I carried bags of clay-breaker, fertilizer, and lime to these places. I planted seeds, and they grew.

I had to carry water to my plants because there was no rain. And I carried more water as the plants grew. It was soon summertime. The sun blazed down, and the wind was scarce in this place. I often didn't carry drinking water for myself. There were times that I almost perished in the heat.

Eventually, it rained. I had planted a marijuana bush in a dry water hole, which began to fill up with water. I waded through a multitude of sexually active cane toads and put my plant in a bucket and took it home. I then began to observe waterflow and its relationship with the earth. This had a far-reaching effect on my thinking.

One day I was climbing down a cliff after it had rained, and I slipped and fell. I fell a long way. The experience of falling seemed like slow motion, as many thoughts went through my mind as I was falling. To my surprise, I landed softly on a bed of lantana. This experience was symbolic of Mother Nature saving my life. In other words, the activity of growing bush-marijuana saved my mind. My average happiness had improved to **6**. I think my happiness would have been higher if I didn't have an unconscious belief that I'd be caught.

I continued to make gardens in the bush. I became familiar with the sound of water lizards, cane toads, kangaroos, hares, pheasants, waterhens and large goannas, as they moved through the bush. That is, I knew what they were without seeing them. I learnt these things quickly (unlike normal industrial tasks). I had found my niche.

The plants grew large through the summer months. I then perceived a change in the air, and the plants perceived it too. It was autumn, and the plants began to bud. And the buds grew large. I pulled the plants out and took them home to dry. I soon had four pounds of dried marijuana buds in my bedroom. I had plants hanging in the boxing shed. I had seedlings growing on the roof because I wanted them to get more sunlight. Autumn wasn't the right season to plant seedlings, but I didn't want to stop growing them. I loved the activity so much.

I also had plants growing in my yard, and they were easy to see. I had become delusional. The police raided me at home. They asked me to show them where I grew the other plants. I took them to the bush and showed them. I guided them around the wasps' nests, along the edges of cliffs, down gullies, and through tunnels made in lantana. I think the police officers enjoyed the experience. But I was sad because my crime was serious. My whole family was sad. It was a dark time in our life.

I waited to be sentenced for my crime. One night I lay in bed with mental energy burning in my head, and there was no outlet. I lay there like a bomb. I finally got up and drove into town. I saw the Ipswich Police Station, and the bomb exploded. I drove around the block while yelling at the police. I stopped outside the police station and walked up the steps.

The police obviously heard me yelling, and they came out to meet me on the steps. The police officers formed a semi-circle around me. They applied various techniques to calm my rage, but they failed. Eventually, an officer advised me to go to the mental health unit at the hospital. This was the right thing to say. I left immediately and went there. I wasn't allowed in the mental health unit, so I yelled out a few words and went home. I had no idea how to fix my mind.

Polly and I waited painfully for my sentencing date. There was a dreadful fear hanging over us. I was afraid of being sent to jail and separated from my family. My family was all I had, and I was afraid of losing that.

My cousins came to visit me during this time. They didn't know about my crime, or my impending court date, or my mental problems. I arrived home and saw my cousins on the veranda, and I started screaming at them. I don't remember what I said, and I don't remember how my cousins reacted. I guess they all went home in shock.

Polly and I continued to wait for my court date. I needed to occupy my mind, and being in the bush was the only option I could see.

I was inspired to write the following poem:

No options here—no options there,
One single option to carry me out of despair.
In the mist of night the animal screams,
Nocturnal butcher-hood in running streams.

Ignoring the shrieking sound of death,
I turned my attention to the left.
I saw a sight that few men see,
No one goes there but security and me.

They'll never find me in the realm I belong,
For my brain is wired for that very song.
But delusion paid for blues to come,
In domestic realms I came undone.

The pain and suffering to come,
It was all worth it.
Alien-ship contained in one,
beyond peoples' understanding.

Chapter 11

Jail

Age: 47

It was now eight months since the cops had raided me. My sentencing date arrived. Polly and I travelled by train to the Brisbane Supreme Court. I had a very good letter from my psychiatrist, and a very good character reference from Jane (the coordinator of the volunteer organisation I worked with). I told my family that these two letters would save me from going to jail.

Polly sat at the back of the courtroom and listened. The prosecutor put forward his statements, and my lawyer put forward his. The prosecutor actually said good things about me. It was now up to the judge. The judge said some introductory words and then announced my sentence. He said, "I sentence you to two years in prison with an automatic parole release in four months". I was then put in the court watch-house, where I fell on my face and cried. I was terrified of being separated from my family. We had never been separated for more than five days, and I always suffered from homesickness on those occasions.

They moved me to the city watch-house that afternoon. I had already committed to the challenge of being separated from my family, but I was worried about Polly. I was worried that she wouldn't cope with the situation. Prisoners were allowed to make one phone call when they arrived at the city watch-house. I asked for my phone call and the officer said, "The call could not get through."

I continually asked for my phone call for the next two days, but I kept getting the same answer: "The call could not get through." I knew Polly would be waiting for me to call her. I was sick from worrying about Polly. Eventually, the call got through, and we cried together on the phone. Polly said, "Going home without you was the hardest thing I ever did." But Polly and I accepted our plight, and we promised each other that we'd be okay.

Prisoners were usually given the medication they needed. I was on thyroxine and ADHD medication. I didn't receive my medication because I had no record to show them. I didn't care about my ADHD medication, but I really needed my thyroxine.

I spent six days in the city watch-house and then I was taken to Arthur Gorrie Correctional Centre. I was confined to my unit in Arthur Gorrie. Each unit consisted of individual prison cells, a guard's office, a kitchen, an eating area, and a small exercise yard. We were allowed to go out of our unit for two hours per week, and we went to the oval on those occasions. I tried to run on the oval, but I injured a calf muscle.

We were locked in our cell for 14 hours at night. This hurt my mind. Some prisoners ate their meals and then went back to their cells. That amazed me. I didn't go back to my cell until I was ordered to go back.

I could see a razor-wire fence from the window of my cell. There was bush behind the fence, and it teased me to see it. But separation from my family was something else; it was sickening. The window of my cell faced towards Ipswich. In my mind, I travelled over the razor-wire fence, through the bush, across the highway, over

Gailes, Goodna, Redbank Plains, across the coal mines to Blackstone, then over Bremer High School, and I looked into our house and saw my family. I wanted to be there.

Each prisoner was given a plate, a bowl, a cup, a knife, a fork and a spoon. We were told not to lose these items because it was hard to replace them. I tried to keep these items together, but I still lost them.

One day we were lining up for dinner, and I realised one of these items was missing. I lost my temper and hit my head about six times with the edge of my plate. Inexperienced prisoners (first timers) were advised not to show their weakness because other prisoners might use it against them. I did show my weakness on that occasion.

We were also advised to keep quiet about our feelings of homesickness. Authorities were concerned that prisoners serving long sentences would harm us if we spoke about our homesickness. I did speak about it. But I didn't *need* to speak about it. Other prisoners just asked me questions and I answered them honestly. I was a very open person. I will elaborate on this openness in the following paragraph.

Being open gave me mental stability. However, it made me different. I knew I was different. I knew this because people seemed to respond strangely when I disclosed things about myself. They seemed to get embarrassed—or something like that. I couldn't understand this because I didn't get embarrassed. I just didn't have that kind of mind. It was hard for me to connect with people.

Being happy in jail seemed to depend on one's ability to socially connect. My family was my only connection to the world. Therefore, I was even lonelier in jail. I started writing this book when I was in Arthur Gorrie. I told the authorities that I was writing a legal letter, which gave me access to a computer. My writing gave me a project to work on, which helped me to bear the loneliness.

I wrote this poem while I was in jail:

> I wait as the time passes by
> The clock moves as the clouds in the sky
> The earth holds secrets of heroes gone by
> Entity in spirit
> Whose eye watches over the hurting
>
> Men in brown pace the pavement
> A journeyman of forty-four has done twenty-five
> He's a gentleman and a pleasure to know
> He sits in his corner and strums his guitar
> He's out in April, a legend by far
>
> There are men in here who look no further
> No further than their current space
> They lost their lives to one single mistake
> I'm looking toward my place
> My place in the arms of Polly
>
> If I'm weak, I'm weak
> If I'm strong, I'm strong
> Nothing matters, as my self-esteem is prolonged
> I'm true to myself and that's my way
> But jail and separation is testing my stay
>
> The razor wire beams silver
> Glistens in the sun
> And the time, and the time, passes by
> And the time, and the time
> Passes by.

We were allowed visitors once a week. I looked forward to seeing Polly and the boys, but parting at the end of visiting times was a sad experience.

It was common for people to get physically fit in prison. However, we had no access to a gym in Arthur Gorrie. Prisoners would do various exercises together. Some big guys did deadlifts with a broomstick loaded with detergent bottles. Some prisoners used punching pads together. A group of prisoners ran circuits inside the unit. I shadow-boxed alone in the exercise yard. I trained very hard in the hot sun.

I had been in Arthur Gorrie for four weeks when a guard approached me and said, "Get your stuff together; you're being shifted to Borallon Correctional Centre". I was loaded into a paddy wagon and taken down the highway to Borallon.

It was better in Borallon. I was now taking my thyroxine tablet, which I really needed. And I had two rocks syringed out of my ears. But the homesickness was punishing me.

We were allowed to go out of our unit now. Prisoners were being moved to different units, and I didn't know why. I found out that I was being moved to a non-worker's unit because I didn't have a job. Apparently, I was supposed to find myself a job. I didn't know this. Non-workers were restricted to their units. I was restricted to my unit at Arthur Gorrie, and I didn't like it. I became very worried about this.

Good news came. A fellow prisoner found me a job washing dishes in the kitchen. I was a worker now. We finished work at about 2.30 pm, and we had to return to our unit by 5.30 pm. This meant that I had three hours to go to the gym or get on a computer and write this book. We then had dinner and were put in our cell for 13 hours.

I attended Alcoholics Anonymous and Narcotics

Anonymous meetings. I wasn't forced to attend these meetings. I voluntarily attended because I was interested in the stories they told. Prisoners would share stories about their lives. I heard many stories about lives that were continuously wrecked by drugs. I don't recommend that people take drugs because some people have addictive personalities. I didn't have an addictive personality.

I'd been at Borallon for two months when a guard approached me and said, "Get your stuff ready; you're leaving for Numinbah straight away". I was then put in a paddy wagon, and we left Borallon. The paddy wagon had a little hole in the back. I looked through this hole as we travelled along the highway. We travelled for one hour and then headed inland toward the mountains. We travelled for another 20 minutes before the car pulled into Numinbah prison. I was allowed out of the car and saw the beautiful green countryside. Numinbah was a cattle farm.

The farm itself covered a large area, but only prisoners who worked with the cattle could go afar. Prisoners like me were restricted to a narrow area that inclined for 500 metres up a mountain. It was a steep incline.

It was much better at Numinbah because we weren't locked up at night. We worked for about five or six hours during the day. I exercised my body after that. I ran several times up the steep incline. I shadow-boxed and lifted weights on alternative days. After exercising, I got on the computer and wrote this book. It was then dinnertime and then showers. We then had a few hours before curfew time. These were the saddest hours of the day. I didn't socialise. I wandered alone from one boundary to the other. My homesickness was really hurting me.

One day I was looking at the road through Numinbah Valley, and I started to cry. I cried because this road led to home. I heard a prisoner coming, and I quickly gathered my composure. I then promised myself that I'd be home soon. I had four weeks to go.

Time passed very slowly, but it did pass. The night before my release had finally come. I was too excited to sleep. Morning came, and a guard asked me to clean my hut. I then went to the administrative area to deal with some matters. I saw Polly in the car park. I was so happy. I was given permission to leave.

Chapter 12

Coaching the Boys for Boxing

Age: 47 to 52

I managed to get a job on a poultry farm when I was released from jail. I thought this job might suit me because I had worked with poultry as a child. However, this job was vastly different to what I expected. This poultry farm sold fertile eggs. I worked in a section that had six sheds, with each shed containing 1,000 roosters and 10,000 hens. The hens laid their eggs in nesting compartments, and these eggs rolled onto a transporting mechanism that transported them to a conveyor belt. Therefore, the eggs of 60,000 hens were transported along this conveyor belt. The workers would sort them according to the size, shape, and quality of their shells.

Sorting the eggs was a major part of the job, and I couldn't do it fast enough. My poor concentration was a problem. I lasted two weeks before I was terminated. I was having the same problem over and over again; I couldn't find a job I was good at.

I applied for a job as a labourer with the local council. I was asked to have a medical examination, so I thought my application was successful. I thought they would ring me and tell me when to start work. However, they rang and told me that my application was unsuccessful. They said I didn't pass the medical examination. I was shocked. I grabbed a piece of wood and bashed into the garden shed.

My family was afraid when they saw me bashing into the garden shed. They were afraid that inactivity would make me crazy again. I spent the next four months trying to find a suitable job, but I failed. I think my happiness averaged about 4 during those four months.

Jason and Tim were involved in competitive boxing. Jason had already competed in 35 amateur fights and six professional fights. Tim had competed in 12 amateur fights by this time. I thought about the idea of presenting our own boxing shows. Presenting boxing shows would give me an interest, which I desperately needed.

Polly and I decided to go ahead with the idea of presenting boxing shows. We needed money to get started. We decided to borrow $50,000. Our plan was to buy a portable boxing ring and use the rest of the money to renovate our house.

We presented an amateur show first. We wanted to gain some experience with amateur shows before we included professional boxers. I advertised in the local paper for people who wanted to have their first fight. Eighteen lads responded. These lads trusted me to match them fairly. Their trust made me feel happy. Tim had a hard fight that night and lost on points. Jason was a professional boxer, so he didn't have an official fight. However, he did have an exhibition bout with a former world champion. We put on a great show, but we lost money.

Our next show consisted of an amateur undercard with one professional fight featuring Jason. I again chose to pre-match all the fights. This time I dealt with boxers who were members of amateur boxing clubs. Pre-matching the fights was a big job because many boxers got sick and pulled out. There was an enormous amount of organising to do, but I managed to get it done. The quality of the entertainment was great. However, we still lost money.

Presenting boxing shows was a family affair. Kristy (my daughter) helped in the canteen. Kristy's husband (James) helped with transporting the boxers. Andy helped Polly on the door and then worked in the canteen later. Jason and Tim helped with various jobs and they also boxed. The shows were always good quality entertainment, but we always lost money.

Our boxing shows also required advertising activities. One of these activities involved towing a sign behind my father's disability buggy. I wore a gorilla suit to draw attention to the sign.

The buggy ran on a battery that went flat at the bottom of a hill. It was a steep hill that continued for one kilometre. I had to get over this hill to get home. I had to take the buggy out of drive mode to remove its compression and then push it up this hill with a heavy trailer attached. It was a hot day, so I took the gorilla suit off my body and hung it on the trailer. I reached the top of the hill, and I decided to free-wheel down the other side. I was enjoying the breeze as I was freewheeling down the hill. The weight of the trailer made me go very fast. I began to wonder where the brakes were. No brakes! Stopping the buggy required the compression to be turned on. The compression was off, and it couldn't be turned on while the machine was moving.

My speed was increasing as I went down the steep hill. I noticed a stop sign ahead. There was barely time to shit myself before I went through the stop sign. I was now approaching a T-junction at the end of the road (with increasing speed).

I thought, will I steer off the road and jump on the grassed footpath, or will I jump out onto the bitumen road? These thoughts were a waste of time as I froze in my seat in fear. I tried to turn the corner at the T-junction, but the machine was too heavy. I crossed the road, hit the gutter, flew off the buggy, and speared into the concrete footpath. I damaged my back in this accident.

We continued to present boxing shows. I always had local lads on the show. Some of these lads had no boxing experience, but I was able to match them with each other. I prided myself on producing fair and entertaining competitions. The workload was enormous. I often became frustrated because I ran out of time. And I verbally expressed my frustration, which made my family uncomfortable.

Jason and Tim also competed in other boxing shows. One time we went to a boxing show that was a two-hour drive from Ipswich. We hired a couple of caravans on this occasion. Tim and his fiancée (Kristy) had arrived early and were settled in their van. Polly and I arrived at the entrance to the caravan park. Polly asked me to go to Tim and Kristy's van and give them a message. She told me to go to a van with a specific number.

I walked through the caravan park, looking for Tim and Kristy's van. I recognised their van's number and walked around the back to enter. There were two vans close together and no numbers on the back. I forgot which van was theirs. I looked into one of the vans, and I saw a person's feet at the end of a bed. I was sure they were Tim's hairy feet, so I walked in. I saw a bikini on the floor, and I thought it was Kristy's. I picked up the bikini and began to put it on (for a joke). Suddenly, the man with hairy feet got off the bed and walked out. It wasn't Tim!

This man was very stern with me. He wanted to know why I was in his van, and why I was putting on his girlfriend's bikini. I told him that I'd made a mistake and I was sorry. He demanded that I leave, and I naturally did.

However, the man became more agitated as I was leaving. I told him again: "I made an honest mistake". The man became verbally aggressive, so I invited him to fight me. He pushed me, and I punched him in the face. He tried to tackle me, and I pushed his head down and hit him with an uppercut. He tried to tackle me again, and I pushed his head down and hit him with another uppercut. He tried again, but this time he pushed me against a park bench. We then began to wrestle.

Tim and Jason were now watching the spectacle. They knew I couldn't wrestle with this fellow because he was big and strong. Tim jumped on his back. The man moved around with Tim on his back. He must have become tired because Jason took over and threw him to the ground quite easily. The man then got up and went away.

I wondered why this fight happened. I wasn't angry with the man. And I didn't have a habit of street fighting. Actually, I was afraid of street fighting. However, I did have a habit of confronting my fear. That's how I overcame OCD. I think the fight happened because I was confronting my fear.

We continued to present boxing shows. I regularly did clown acts on our shows. I had bought a blow-up doll from an adult shop, and I sometimes used it for clowning purposes. It was a female. I dressed the blow-up doll in a nightdress and had it carried to the ring on a stretcher. The ringside doctor was told to examine it and pronounce it "dead". The departed doll was then taken away, and the program continued. I later came out to the boxing ring wearing boxing gloves and a fake nose. Meanwhile, two people dressed in gorilla suits pushed a wheelie bin out to the ring. The wheelie bin was painted like a coffin.

A girl by the name of Debbie Schubert came out of

the wheelie bin wearing the blow-up doll's nightdress (i.e., the blow-up doll had come back to life). Debbie had boxing gloves on, and I pretended to fight with her. Ten people dressed in black clothes entered the ring, and a brawl broke out. Grim reapers, gorillas and clowns of all kinds were involved. I think most people liked it.

We had presented six shows in Ipswich by now. Organising the shows was difficult because of my poor concentration. I did most of the work because Polly, Jason and Tim were working, and Andy was still at school. It took one month to prepare for a show, and we averaged one show every three months. I was generally happy, except for the month leading up to the shows. It was better when the shows were finished, and I could think about the next show without time constraints. Presenting boxing shows gave me a purpose in my life, and my happiness was averaging **6.5**.

I planned to hold our seventh show in Brisbane, which is 50 km east of Ipswich. I thought we'd draw a big crowd in Brisbane. Tim was now a professional boxer. I decided to have five professional fights because I thought a full professional program would create more interest. Paying for five professional fights was a big financial risk. Polly and the boys didn't want to take that risk, but I wouldn't listen to them. I was determined to make it work.

Showtime arrived. The program started and the crowd wasn't there. I kept checking to see if people were coming in the door, but the people didn't come. We lost $7,000 that night. That was a big loss for us because we weren't resourceful people. Polly and the boys refused to be involved in any more boxing shows. I felt absolutely destroyed.

I had little to do after the Brisbane show. I was bored, resentful, and angry. I decided to cultivate a vegetable garden in a paddock. I grew lettuce, broccoli, cabbage, and onions. It was winter, and I covered the vegetables with clear plastic to prevent them from being frosted. I could have grown the vegetables at home, but this wouldn't help my mind. You see, doing it on private property was like growing marijuana. Of course, growing marijuana was more interesting.

The paddock in which I grew the vegetables was slashed regularly, but my garden was hidden on a little hill. The slasher didn't go there. And I thought the slasher driver would avoid my garden if he did decide to go there. Just as my vegetables started to ripen, the slasher went up on the hill and cut my little garden down. I was angry and resentful. I wasn't angry about losing my vegetables. I was angry because my boxing business was taken from me.

It was now two months since my vegetables were slashed. Polly and I went for walks in the bush, but I wanted more than that. I wanted something to occupy my mind. I decided to present an amateur show. My family approved because amateur shows were not a financial risk.

I had learnt things from the previous shows. I learnt that some tasks were a waste of time and money. Therefore, I didn't do as much work for this show. Anyway, showtime arrived, and it all went well. Our shows always went well on the night. However, I didn't find a purpose in this show because Jason and Tim didn't have a proper contest because they were professional boxers.

I wanted to do one more amateur/professional show. I wanted to prove to my family that I could be efficient and economical. However, Polly and the boys were affected by our previous loss of money and my acts of frustration. They didn't want to do any more shows. We had presented boxing shows for the past two years, and my happiness averaged **6.5** during that time.

My happiness dropped to about 3. I decided to grow some corn in a place that was guarded by security. I tried to make myself happy through this activity. Unfortunately, I damaged my knee and couldn't nurture the corn. My happiness dropped to 2. I felt sad because my boxing business was taken from me.

Jason and Tim continued to box on other shows, and my happiness did improve. They both fought for various titles and did well. My time was only partly occupied now, and my happiness averaged 4.5.

I was then offered a cleaning job at an abattoir. I knew my poor concentration would affect my work performance, but I wanted to try. I had to attend an induction course before I could start. I usually had trouble with induction courses because the content was covered so quickly. I told the teacher about my concentration problem, and he slowed down for me.

I got through the induction course and then received on-the-job training. My job was to clean a big complex machine. There were many things to remember. I went home and rehearsed these things to remember them. I really tried hard. I struggled with this job for one week before I was terminated. I just couldn't meet the standard. This experience helped me to understand myself better. That is, I realised exactly how poor my rote-learning ability was. And more importantly, I realised that my visual memory was extremely poor. I was still learning about my disabilities.

It was now the beginning of 2011, and a great flood came. The flood of 2011 was a spike on my chart of happiness. Polly was on holiday at the time, and we went out at night to watch the waters rise. We were often by ourselves in the dark. We caught eels in the rivers and creeks (just like my childhood days). After I caught an eel, I'd take all my clothes off and speak in a foreign accent. This was a risk because there was a chance that someone could arrive and be offended. I often took risks like this. I felt alive when I took these risks.

Tim had two more fights after the flood and then stopped boxing. Jason had four more fights and stopped. The boys had boxed for two-and-a-half years after we finished presenting our own shows. My happiness averaged **4.5** during those two-and-a-half years. My involvement with boxing was now completely finished. And my happiness dropped dramatically.

Chapter 13

What Could I Do to Occupy My Mind?

Age: 52 to 55

I always needed a strong challenge in my life. I needed something intense to do. I was naturally intense. I was intense when I interacted with people. That is, I enjoyed talking about deep and meaningful things or bizarre nonsense. People usually didn't talk like that, so most people avoided me. With very few friends, no job, and no hobby, I had very little to occupy my mind. Therefore, negative thoughts occupied my mind.

I spent all day by myself while Polly was at work. We watched television together at night, but that wasn't intense enough for me. Polly went to bed at midnight, and I stayed up by myself. Sometimes I'd walk down my street and speak loudly to the people who were in their houses (probably sleeping). I'd become angry, and I'd end up yelling at the people who were sleeping in their houses. It was now two months since boxing had finished, and my happiness was averaging **3**.

Polly tried to make me happy. We went for walks in the bush because she knew I liked doing that. But I liked to cross boundaries. I liked walking through private property because the challenge occupied my mind. Polly didn't want to do this. There were several reasons why she didn't want to do it. The most obvious reason was that she didn't feel comfortable with this kind of intensity. But I wish to mention something new here. That is, she could not do certain mental activities that I could do. I will explain this in the following paragraph.

I could mentally process:

- The distance between the property owners and myself, and the obstructions in the property owner's line of view; and
- the distance those obstructions were from the property owners (and the fact that the obstruction would appear magnified if it was close to the viewers' eyes);
- I was aware of the colour of my clothes, and if I was moving or not moving;
- I could assess the chance of the property owners' attention being directed toward me (which was often based on the activity they were engaged with); and
- I could calculate the probability of comforting property owners if I was seen.

I had a good track record of doing these things when I was in the bush. Polly wasn't good at these mental activities, and she probably couldn't understand that I was. Therefore, we didn't walk through private property.

I wanted to challenge myself. And the degree of challenge in my life was very small. It was now six months since boxing had finished. My happiness was averaging about **4**. I continued to have periods of anger and sadness.

There were organisations that helped disabled people to find employment. They were called Disability Employment Agencies. I joined one of these, and my case worker was a mental health professional. However, the organisation couldn't begin helping me until my details were processed. I had to wait.

While I was waiting, I began thinking about my brain, and how it worked. I realised that I could hyper-focus. I will explain this "hyper-focusing" according to my experience.

The next six paragraphs are complex and may need to be read more than once.

My brain is hyperactive. Therefore, I can hyper-focus, but only if I can maintain my concentration. I can perform very well on a task if I can maintain my concentration. It's like a fast dog running on a slippery surface, versus a non-slippery surface. I'm like the fast dog. A fast dog will perform well if it can maintain its traction. However, fast dogs tend to lose traction on certain surfaces. Likewise, people with fast brains can lose their concentration on certain tasks. Therefore, my ability to maintain concentration depends on the type of task.

So then, what type of task can I maintain my concentration on? There is an idea that people with ADHD need to be interested in the task to maintain their concentration. The truth is, being interested in the task makes little difference to me because I'm very determined. So then, what type of task can I maintain my concentration on? I will explain this in the next four paragraphs.

Snap is a card game where each player takes turns dealing cards onto a pile. The players quickly place their non-dealing hand on the pile of cards when a pair appears in succession. Therefore, the task is to grab the pile of cards before the other players can grab them. Hence, the game is sometimes called "grab" as well. I was good at this task, but only 50% of the time. My performance went from good to poor as my concentration slipped in and out. This is like a fast dog running on a semi-slippery surface.

Sorting eggs on the egg farm was a difficult task for me (see Chapter 12). I had to distinguish between the different sizes, shapes, and textures of eggs, and I had to sort them accordingly. This task was like a fast dog running on a slippery surface. My brain went too fast to get traction on that task. My brain went too fast to get traction on most tasks in the workplace. I couldn't remember the names of things because my thoughts went too fast to rote learn. I had poor visual memory because my thoughts went too fast for visual information to gel. My thoughts *flowed*. Therefore, I was extremely good at tasks that required *flowing thought processes*.

So then, what type of tasks require flowing thought processes? It is the type of task that doesn't require previous thoughts to be retained. It is the type of task that only requires a conclusion. I am good at considering things that exist outside the box. I'm good at identifying confounding variables within psychological research. While my photographic memory is extremely poor, I can visualise what other people see. I can assume the thoughts of other drivers when I drive my car. I can maintain my focus on these tasks because they require flowing thought processes. That's when I can hyper-focus. I hyper-focus because my brain is fast/intense. My fast brain *propels* my thoughts to the next thought, and the next, and the next, until the conclusion is reached. That's why I can't remember my previous thoughts.

I would thrive in a prehistoric environment, but I do have problems in this modern world. There's too much reading and rote learning required now. There are computer operations, rules to learn, and forms to fill out. This is all rote learning. My brain doesn't perform well in this modern world.

My psychological condition wasn't the only issue affecting my working capacity. My body had also been damaged, and I also had a criminal record. Therefore, getting a job would be difficult. So how could I get a job? I mentioned above that I joined a Disability Employment Agency, but it couldn't begin helping me until my details were processed.

My details were now processed. These details included three barriers to gaining employment. My psychiatrist had mentioned these barriers in his referral to the Disability Employment Agency. These three barriers were:

1. Little or no friendship/support network (other than immediate family);

2. Social isolation;

3. Episodes of negative emotions that fluctuated in times of stress.

I didn't want these barriers mentioned in the referral, and I was upset about it.

Some time went by. The Disability Employment Agency didn't seem to be helping me. I thought my case worker was rejecting me. I thought the whole world was rejecting me. I spoke to my case worker about transferring to another agency, and she organised that for me. Now I had to wait for the new agency to begin helping me. All I seemed to do was wait. Thoughts of discrimination arose in my mind as I waited. My happiness dropped from 4 to **3**.

I knew that people got jobs through their friends. That is, I knew we lived in a world that required networking. I did know someone who could refer me to an employer, but this person wouldn't help me. I was very disappointed that nobody in this world would help me. I believed a spiritual network was trying to destroy me.

One day I was thinking about this spiritual network

and my mind exploded. At that moment, I looked for something to damage. Amidst this fit of rage, I saw a woman's night dress lying on the floor. I put it on and drove into town. I walked around town in the nightdress, and I felt better. I felt there was something to learn from this experience, but I didn't know what it was.

I continued to suffer from episodes of anger. Polly and I had a serious talk about my anger problem, as we were trying to understand it. We agreed that I didn't fit into the world. I told Polly that I couldn't connect with people because I didn't share an interest with them. However, Polly believed my problem was more serious than that. She believed my communication was chronically negative. She argued that my negative communication was preventing me from gaining access to institutions. Well, I was frustrated because I couldn't fit into the world.

I tried to stop speaking negatively, and I achieved it for a few days. However, I soon became bored, and my negative communication returned. This relapse affected me immediately. I immediately gave up the desire to have a job (or a normal project). At that moment, I realised why I felt better when I wore a woman's dress in public. I realised that clowning could replace a normal project. In other words, I didn't need to fear inactivity. Therefore, giving up this desire reduced my fear. With this, my happiness increased from 3 to **4.5**.

Jason told me about a cleaning job that was available. I applied for the job and was accepted. Interestingly, I got this job when I gave up the desire to have one. I worked three shifts per week, and each shift was two hours long. I cleaned the floor of a shop, a kitchen, a toilet, and a manager's office. I performed okay at this job. My happiness increased by two; it was now **6.5**. I continued with this job for eight months, and my happiness remained the same.

I then experienced something that really upset me. I don't wish to explain the situation because it will affect other people's privacy. Anyway, my happiness dropped very low (it was probably **1**). I expressed my anger differently this time. I had fits of anger when I was driving my car. That is, I flipped out and did dangerous things for 15 seconds, and then I returned to normal driving. I had never experienced such a loss of control. Maybe this happened because I tried so hard to *maintain* control.

There is something important to mention about the above-stated flip-outs. That is, my precision and timing were excellent in this state of heightened rage. Maybe this is related to my ability to function at high levels of intensity.

Anyway, my emotional suffering continued. I was still doing the cleaning job, but my back and shoulder became sore. The accident with my father's buggy had caused problems with my back. I chose to quit the job because I wanted to look after my health. Quitting the job meant that I didn't need to drive to work. This was good because something bad would have happened.

I was mentally unwell. My old church had taught me that stumbling blocks were steppingstones to greater wisdom. That always helped me, and it probably helped me this time. My happiness improved to **3** after a few months.

Although my happiness improved a bit, my negative belief had grown. It was a very dark belief. I believed a spiritual network would make everyone reject me. I half-believed that this spiritual network would drive me to suicide. My thoughts were very intimidating.

It was now 15 months since boxing had finished. Tim was still working in the mines, but he was becoming bored. He started to go to the gym after work, and he asked me to train him for a couple of fights. Naturally, I was happy to do this. Tim came home from the mines every second week, and we trained together on those occasions. This activity improved my happiness from 3 to 5. However, my paranoia had grown. I didn't trust the world anymore.

Tim left the mines and found a job in Ipswich. I now trained Tim every second day, which was good. He had a fight and won. He then had another fight and lost to a talented boxer. Losing never worried me much. I just loved to be involved in something. Actually, I thought my involvement with boxing was necessary to dissolve my belief in this spiritual network. However, there was a problem: Tim wanted to quit boxing. I asked him to have one more fight. I thought this would help to dissolve my dark belief. Tim agreed to do this.

Meanwhile, I noticed that Polly's tolerance to stress had decreased. The doctor said she was going through menopause. This made me think about Polly and what she had done in her life. She had given her heart to her children, and then went to work when our last child started kindergarten. Furthermore, she had dealt with my mental issues for the last 10 years. I really wanted to overcome my mental issues (for Polly's sake).

Polly had always wanted to travel overseas. We saved some money and planned to visit Fiji. Polly was excited about our planned holiday. I was determined to control my behaviour and give Polly a good holiday.

The time for our holiday came. We travelled to Fiji. We got off the plane and were greeted by Fijians who were singing and playing musical instruments. We hired a car and travelled around the island.

I controlled my behaviour while I was in Fiji because I didn't want to offend the Fijians. This left me with unused mental energy, which was a problem. I also couldn't sleep at night, which made things worse. I became emotional on three occasions during our holiday and had arguments with Polly. However, we recovered quickly from these arguments. I really tried hard to make our holiday enjoyable (for Polly's sake).

Polly said that she enjoyed her holiday. I was happy with myself for not spoiling it. Some people may think that I shouldn't be happy with myself. That is, I should expect more of myself. However, I didn't need to follow the ideas of people because I was always honest with myself.

We returned to Australia. I received a phone call from a boxing promoter who needed an opponent for a world-rated fighter in two days. Tim accepted the fight, and he lost by a points decision. That was Tim's "one more fight". I didn't think this fight would happen so quickly. I still believed a spiritual network was trying to destroy me. I needed to prove to myself that it wasn't true. I needed Tim to have another fight, as this would indicate to me that the spiritual network was allowing me to integrate with the world. Tim agreed to have another fight.

It was around this time that I had an experience with a man who suffered from OCD. We spoke about deep and meaningful things. I wanted to spend more time with this man, but he couldn't give me that time. I thought deeply about why people didn't have time for me. My thoughts are explained in the following paragraphs.

I had plenty of friends when I suffered from OCD. But I seemed to have lost my ability to have friends. It seemed like I had changed somehow. I wanted to understand how and why I had changed. Therefore, I asked myself the following question: How was this man (with OCD) different from me? Well, it seemed like he was different in the same way that society was different from me. That is, people seem to need a common way to think. This is culture, or collective ideas. I really didn't identify with any culture or collective ideas. Why was I like this? I tried to answer this question. My answer follows.

People with OCD seem to use their mental energy to convince themselves of things. I used my mental energy to convince myself of the content of my previous thoughts. But I was no longer tortured by compulsions, so maybe this left me with unused mental energy. And maybe I used this mental energy to question collective ideas. However, I believed there was more to it than that. The truth is, I didn't know why I couldn't identify with any culture.

I asked myself another question: What about other people who overcome OCD; what do they do with their mental energy? Do they question collective thinking? Well, they might. However, they probably don't because it would affect their social life. Therefore, their mental energy may be used in other ways. Some might take risks like people with ADHD do. Others might have TS symptoms. I used my mental energy with ADHD and TS symptoms.

Was I more ADHD, or TS? Well, I *can* answer this question. It depended on my mood. I had two basic moods: a non-thinking mood, and a thinking mood. I will explain my non-thinking mood first.

My non-thinking mood was more relaxed than my thinking mood. My mental energy would startle me when I was in a non-thinking mood (because I was relaxed). There was no pre-second planning about what I would say or do. Therefore, my behaviour would burst out of me. I'd express vulgar words, bizarre words, or jerky movements (i.e., TS symptoms).

My thinking mood was not so relaxed. That is, the mental energy did not startle me because I was prepared to express something (I was thinking). Hence, I expressed silly concepts and bizarre ideas (i.e., ADHD symptoms).

In summary, my different moods would give rise to

different symptoms (either ADHD or TS symptoms). I often told people about my ADHD because I didn't want them to judge me negatively. However, they still did. I then discovered a better way to help people understand me. I'd tell them that I had TS, and I expressed it by saying silly concepts and bizarre ideas. I then asked them not to be offended if I did this. I found that people could understand this, and they didn't judge me negatively. Well, saying silly concepts and bizarre ideas is more like ADHD symptoms. However, my arousal theory permitted me to say that it was TS.

Anyway, my happiness had averaged **5** since Tim started boxing again. My involvement with boxing helped me to be happy. However, I still experienced periods of sadness because I knew Tim wanted to stop boxing. I felt insecure. And my chronic paranoia made everything worse.

Tim had one more fight and then stopped boxing. I was hoping to establish a connection with the world through Tim's boxing. This didn't happen. I still believed a spiritual network was trying to destroy me.

I now had nothing to do again. My happiness dropped to **3**. I was intimidated by dark thoughts. I was afraid my family would abandon me, and I needed them to reassure me. It was hard for them to give me this reassurance because they couldn't understand why I needed it. And I couldn't explain why I needed it because I didn't fully understand it myself. However, a couple of months went by, and I grew to understand my problem. I could then explain it to my family, and they were able to give me reassurance and support me better.

My family's support helped me. I started to think of options to occupy my mind. I thought of three options. One option was to register with the Disability Employment Service (again). Another option was to attend a TS support group, with the intention to find a friend. My third option was to attend a Buddhist institution and study Buddhism. I was always interested in Buddhism, but I had never studied it properly.

I started to apply these options. I registered with a Disability Employment Service, but I encountered problems. I decided to abandon that option. I then decided to contact a TS support group. I went to a support group meeting, which was attended by two families who had young children with TS. I really wanted to socialise with adults who had TS. It seemed like the TS support group wasn't going to provide that opportunity. I decided to abandon that option also. I then decided to attend a Buddhist organisation.

Chapter 14

Attention Diverted to a Higher Dimension

Age: 55 to 60

We attended a Buddhist temple. The temple held meditation classes and provided lessons on Buddhism. The lessons were held at four levels, and Polly and I enrolled in the level one course.

We went to the temple every Sunday. I soon learnt that meditation is an essential part of Buddhist teaching. I also learnt that meditation involved concentration. We were shown different ways to meditate. There was walking meditation, breathing meditation, mantras and Tai Chi. Tai Chi is a form of physical movement where participants focus their concentration on their body as they move it. Walking meditation was like Tai Chi, but the body movement involved walking, and they concentrated on that. The mantras involved repeating words and concentrating on their pronunciation. I liked the breathing meditation, which involved concentrating on the air going through our airways as we inhaled, and on counting our breaths as we exhaled. We counted from zero to 10, and then backwards from 10 to zero.

Breathing meditation allowed me to observe my concentration. I detected *minor* interferences in my concentration during every breath. I call them minor interferences because I didn't lose count of my breaths. I also had *major* interferences in my concentration, which *did* make me lose count of my breaths. Apparently, it was normal for beginners to lose count of their breaths. However, I didn't know if it was normal to have these minor interferences.

I am now writing about the period in which I am currently living. Therefore, I am a novice meditator, and my writing may reflect this.

I learnt about the benefits of meditation. I learnt that meditation would make me happier. I learnt to focus on the split-second of the present moment. I learnt that thoughts about the past or future would arise if I didn't focus on the present second. I also understood that thinking excessively about the past and future was not good for my mind. This made a lot of sense to me. And it made more sense when I practised meditation.

Polly and I continued to go to the temple on Sundays. I liked learning about Buddhism, and I was keen to practise meditation at home. However, dark thoughts often prevented me from practising at home. I really believed that meditation would heal my mind, but I would need to practise more.

It took six weeks to complete the level one course. Polly and I decided to repeat level one. It was normal for students to repeat the courses.

I was determined to meditate more at home. I needed to meditate before the dark thoughts prevented me from doing it. I vowed to myself that I would do this.

Meanwhile, I needed to do some work on our house. I needed to deal with drainage, fix plumbing, and replace house stumps and other things. Polly was worried that I couldn't do these jobs. We had serious arguments about this. I wanted to do these jobs because I wanted to be useful. Eventually, we agreed that I would do the work.

I had to ask people how to do certain jobs. People wouldn't return my phone calls, which made me paranoid. Paranoia was now an added factor in my dark belief. That is, I believed a spiritual network was trying to destroy me. This belief incorporated certain thoughts. I thought everyone would abandon me. And I thought Polly would abandon me. I had episodes of darkness that lasted for two days. I had one day of anger, followed by one day of depression. This happened twice a week. I'd had four days of darkness every week for the last nine years, and I'd had severe paranoia for the last two years.

Sometimes I didn't work on the house for months. My dark thoughts weren't the only thing that held up my work. Sometimes I wasn't sure what to do, so I had to wait for a plan to gel in my mind. However, I maintained my determination to do these jobs. I eventually removed our concrete boxing ring and removed trees and untidy gardens. I had to remove the trees and gardens to fix other things.

I continued to work on the house, and I also continued to learn about Buddhism and meditation. I learnt that attachments (i.e., things we love) interfere with my concentration during meditation. I wondered if my high arousal affected my concentration during meditation. However, I was told that my performance was normal, so maybe it didn't.

Polly and I completed the level one course for the second time, and we also completed level two. It was now nine months since I began studying Buddhism. My meditation practice had increased to an average of 40 minutes per day.

Practising meditation affected me in the following ways:

- My comfort during meditation improved.
- My concentration during meditation improved.
- My overall happiness improved by two units (it was now **5**).
- My paranoia did not improve.

So why did my overall happiness improve, but my paranoia did not? Perhaps my newly found practice gave me hope, and maybe this hope made me happier. Although my happiness was averaging **5**, I was still experiencing episodes of darkness.

Another two months went by. Polly and I had now completed level two for the second time. I think my happiness dropped a little. Regardless, I still had a strong belief that practising meditation would help my mind. This belief remained strong in the face of recurring anger and depression. I just believed my practice had to increase. My practice had to be more than a scheduled activity; it had to be an activity that did not cease.

Polly and I began the level three course. I was inspired to be more confident in my judgement of things. This inspiration enabled me to better understand the Buddhist teaching. I understood that no individual was separate from the universe. I had created my separate self through thinking. In other words, I had created my identity through thinking. This better understanding was still just a theory, but the theory seemed clearer now.

I still suffered from fear-based paranoia and periods of darkness. Actually, my average happiness dropped to **3**. Polly and I were arguing a lot. I was afraid that Polly would abandon me, although she didn't say this. I needed to meditate all the time to stop these dark thoughts.

I began to integrate meditation with my daily activities. That is, I began to apply my full attention to activities that didn't require my full attention. I managed to increase my practice, but I still wasn't meditating all the time. Dark thoughts would arise when I wasn't meditating. I knew my paranoia initiated these dark thoughts. Buddhism had taught me that negative thoughts become stronger if I entertain them. In other words, too much thinking makes me a compulsive thinker. I needed to think less. I continued to arrive at the same answer. Meditation was the answer.

I began to listen to spiritual teachers on YouTube. I began to broaden my view on meditation. I began to call it "presence". This word appealed to me because it implied that meditation could be a natural activity. That is, I could fully concentrate on activities that didn't require my full concentration.

I had some success at integrating presence with my natural activities. However, dark thoughts continued to arise when I wasn't present. My average happiness was about 3 or 4.

I then had an accident and hurt my knee. I was placed on a waiting list to have surgery. One day I was exercising my sore knee in a swimming pool. I was moving my leg at the highest possible intensity without feeling pain. I also maintained relaxation in the muscles I wasn't using. This required concentration. It was an ideal way to be present. I finished this activity and began thinking about the Buddhist teaching. My thoughts seemed to be unblocked. I suddenly had a clearer understanding of the abovementioned "separate self". This experience was so profound that my dark episodes stopped. I thought my mental illness was finally healed. My dark thoughts stopped for two weeks. I then had an argument with Polly, and my dark thoughts returned. Obviously, my mental illness was not healed. This relapse made me think more deeply about my problem. This is explained below.

Firstly, what was my problem? Well, there were many problems. I was bored and wanted a job; I was lonely; I thought Polly would abandon me; I thought everyone would abandon me. However, all these problems were parts of one bigger problem: I believed a spiritual network was trying to destroy me. This spiritual network was not a particular institution. It was the world itself; I thought the world was trying to destroy me.

I concluded that I could not change my thoughts because I'd be discarding my judgement. I needed my judgement. So, what should I do? I should stop thinking. Therefore, I needed to be present. I had come to the same conclusion again.

I thought it was time to assess my practice. I wanted to be *absolutely* sure that meditation (presence) was helping me. Wanting to be absolutely sure was a mild obsession. However, I didn't have compulsions anymore. So how did I process this mild obsession without having compulsions? My mental processing is explained in the following three paragraphs.

So then, how could I be absolutely sure that practising presence was helping me? Well, I needed to compare my current situation with the past. I remembered a type of meditation I had practised in the past. That is, I would lie in bed and focus my attention on a dot on the ceiling. I don't recommend this type of meditation, but I did it in the early stages of my practice because I didn't know any better. Anyway, I remembered how I felt when I focused on the dot. Therefore, I decided to do it again and compare the two feelings.

I focused on this dot, and I felt more comfortable. However, I didn't think this was enough to justify a conclusion (i.e., absolute surety). I then looked out the window at various things. Things seemed better to look at now. However, I wanted to be sure that I wasn't lying to myself. I decided to analyse the conditions of my life. I then realised that I didn't suffer from boredom anymore. It was the first time I had realised this. I was then absolutely sure that practising presence was helping me.

So, I had reached the conclusion that practising presence was helping me. However, I still believed that a spiritual network was trying to destroy me. I still had issues with anger and paranoia. Therefore, I was not free from this mental illness.

Polly wanted me to get help with this mental illness. I agreed to do this. We found an organisation that helped people with mental illness. I joined this organisation, and a support worker was provided for me. I told the support worker that I practiced presence, and it helped me. I told him that I wanted to help others to practise. The support worker asked me to facilitate a meditation class within this organisation. I gladly accepted this task.

I'm calling it meditation (not presence) because that is how I communicated to people within the organisation.

I began facilitating a meditation class with a paid worker watching. The participants were happy with the class, and the manager of the organisation seemed happy with my work. I did more than facilitate sessions of meditation. I explained the benefits of meditation because I wanted the participants to practise at home. I also referred to teachers on YouTube. I also explained the importance of fully concentrating on daily tasks. That is, those daily tasks that are usually considered to be boring. I explained how my chronic boredom had dissolved over time.

Not only had my boredom dissolved, but my desire to have an occupation was gone. Furthermore, my desire to have friends had reduced. However, I still thought a spiritual network was trying to destroy me. Therefore, I still had some mental issues.

I had now been facilitating the meditation class for a few months. The participants seemed very happy with the class. And I was happy because I was doing something useful. One day the manager told me that she wasn't happy with my work. This was strange because the manager *was* previously happy with my work. Nothing really changed with the sessions. In fact, I think the participants were becoming even happier with the sessions. It wasn't long before I was stopped from facilitating the class. I was disappointed. What could I do? All I could do was continue practising. And that's what I did.

I was still working on our house. One day I lifted something heavy in a confined space. My back became stiff, and I experienced horrific pain in my hip. The pain was so bad that Polly called an ambulance, and I was taken to hospital. The doctor wanted to keep me in the hospital, but I opted to come home with painkillers. I had two more trips to the hospital over the next two weeks. I couldn't stand up for more than two minutes. I was bedridden. I then had an MRI, which revealed a badly bulged disk. I was referred to a neurosurgeon who performed emergency surgery within the public system.

There was also evidence of a compression fracture in my thoracic spine. This happened 12 years ago when I crashed my father's pensioner buggy. These two injuries prevented me from lifting heavy weights.

More time went by. I became sick in my lower stomach. I was diagnosed with a bowel infection. My bowel ruptured, and my condition was life-threatening. I was admitted to the hospital for six days where I received various antibiotics through a drip. I mention these physical conditions because they were relevant to my mental condition. I was surprised how well I accepted these physical conditions. I believe that practising presence helped me to do this. However, my episodes of darkness continued.

I had now been practising presence for three-and-a-half years. I had finished all four levels at the temple. I was now visiting other Buddhist organisations and listening to various spiritual teachers on YouTube. Practising presence was more important to me than Buddhism.

Despite my diligence in practicing presence, I still believed a spiritual network was trying to destroy me. I continued to fear that everyone would abandon me, and that Polly would also abandon me. I had to let go of my dysfunctional attachment to Polly. I knew I would eventually do this through practising presence. I had an unshakable belief that my dark thoughts would cease. It seemed strange that my belief in practising presence remained so strong when I repeatedly failed. But that's how it was.

Another year passed, and I became ill with another bowel infection. This time I was passing blood. I was placed on a waiting list to have a colonoscopy. The bleeding became worse as I waited for this medical procedure.

I eventually had the colonoscopy and it revealed "ulcerative colitis". This is a bowel disease that periodically flares up. I was referred to another hospital to receive drug treatment, but I had to wait. I eventually received the treatment, and it helped me. Again, I was surprised how well I accepted this physical condition.

I had been practising presence for five years now. I encountered various organisations and listened to various teachers on YouTube. My mind had healed a lot during those five years. I didn't suffer from boredom anymore. I was spending a lot of time alone and I wasn't suffering from loneliness. I no longer cared about having a job. And, I no longer believed a spiritual network was trying to destroy me. My episodes of darkness had reduced to one per month. My happiness was now averaging about 7.

I was now finding it hard to write. Maybe I thought there wasn't much to write about. Maybe I was tired of writing about myself. But I knew my writing wasn't finished yet. Therefore, I decided to write some fiction and continue my report later.

Chapter 15

Attention Diverted to a Higher Dimension and To Stillness

Age: 62 to 64

Two years went by while I wrote a fiction story. My happiness continued to improve during that time. I no longer set aside time for practising presence. I just enjoyed being present during normal activities.

I was the happiest I'd ever been during my adult life. However, I still had challenges in my life. My challenges were usually related to my inability to rote learn. I would fail to do things and I'd become frustrated. Sometimes there were consequences to my failure, and I'd become angry and headbutt things. But this anger didn't qualify as episodes of darkness because it passed quickly.

So why did I headbutt things when I got frustrated? Well, the type of behaviour (headbutting) was just a habit. But my frustration was fuelled by surges of arousal. And the intensity of the behaviour was also fuelled by arousal. If you observe the intensity of TS symptoms, you can understand how this could happen.

Anyway, I experienced three heavy head knocks in a short time. Two were self-inflicted and one was an accident. I suffered severe headaches after my last head knock, and the doctor ordered an MRI. There was no structural damage, but a "medical condition" was reported. The doctor referred me to a neurologist.

I had to wait for my appointment with the neurologist. While I was waiting, I began looking at this medical condition on the internet. I was shocked. Apparently, I could expect a fast decline in memory and to die of a stroke within five years. I searched the internet for more information, but everything I found was the same.

It was now three weeks since my last head knock, and my headaches were terrible. I was also experiencing dizziness, which constantly reminded me that a stroke was coming. The idea of dying in five years was disappointing. I wanted to do certain things before I died. I wanted to finish this book and finish working on the house. I tried to talk to Polly about my impending death. I wanted to prepare her for it. However, Polly didn't want to talk about it. She wanted to talk to the neurologist first.

It was now five weeks since my last head knock. My dizziness had started to improve. It was now time for my appointment. The neurologist heard my story and viewed the MRI scans. He said the results of the MRI did not suggest that I would die soon. This was very good news. I gained spiritual benefits from having to accept a perceived death sentence. In other words: I let go of a significant source of suffering. Two more weeks passed, and my dizziness was completely gone.

I spoke to my daughter-in-law (Kristy) about my inability to rote learn and my headbutting behaviour. She suggested that I apply for help through a disability agency. I was successful with this application and an occupational therapist began teaching me things.

I was taught to set alarms on my smart phone, which helped me to keep appointments. I was also taught to use a navigation application on my smart phone. I learnt to use the washing machine, which saved Polly some work. I learnt to use a parking meter, but I failed to remember that. I could learn these things because the occupational therapist took extra time to teach me. I learnt many things that were related to modern living.

More time went by. I had been practising presence for eight years now. I haven't been rating my happiness in this chapter. This is because presence produced a different kind of happiness. My previous happiness involved occupying the mind. Presence did not involve the mind. But this is according to a specific definition of the mind. I will explain this definition below.

The brain is flesh, and it can be physically observed. This mind I'm referring to is spirit, and it cannot be physically observed. This mind is conditioned by passionate thinking. In other words, our love and hate for things *evolve* with every passionate thought. Sooner or later, our love and hate for things will manifest in emotional suffering. Therefore, this mind is the source of emotional suffering. We fear loss in the *future*. And we resent our losses from the *past*. But we can transcend this mind through practising *presence*.

I will discuss the brain now. I mentioned in Chapter 8 that some people with these three disorders may *not* have high arousal. Therefore, I believe it is important to test patients for high arousal, so patients can receive specific treatment.

How do you test for high arousal? I believe high arousal can be identified with a test that measures poor concentration (i.e., second-by-second attention deficit). I believe this is the only symptom of the three disorders that is *caused* by high arousal. The other symptoms are merely *energised* by it. This is why measuring second-by-second attention deficit will identify high arousal.

What is the ideal treatment for problematic high

arousal? I'm not qualified to discuss treatments, but I can hypothesise. I *think* my arousal became less intense from practising presence. I'm *sure* my arousal became less intense when my severe compulsions ceased. Both these life changes involved a reduction of intense mental activities (i.e., stress). This may be just my experience, but it *is* reasonable to suggest that practising intense mental activities would create an intense brain (i.e., high arousal). Therefore, **I hypothesise that refraining from intense mental activities and practising presence is the ideal treatment for high arousal.** This research project should be conducted over a long time because brain arousal can be semi-permanent.

Something else needs to be said before this book is finished. I dealt with OCD by doing what I wanted to do (regardless of fear). This conditioned me to live according to my conclusions without knowing how I derived them. But this *conditioning* created an unusual personality, which led to social problems. And then I couldn't occupy my mind, which increased my social problems. This leaves us with a question: How should other people deal with their OCD symptoms?

I wish to remind the reader that I am not qualified to advise anyone about treatments for any disorder. However, let's think about OCD symptoms. Let's imagine that two components contribute to OCD symptoms. Let's say that some sufferers have *higher arousal* causing their symptoms, and others have more *basic anxiety* causing their symptoms. In other words, each sufferer has various amounts of these two components.

OCD sufferers with higher arousal: I believe high arousal is the ADHD part of OCD (see Chapter 8). This is when the attention deficit (second-by-second) affects the working memory (see Chapter 13). People with OCD might complete a simple task, but they have a hazy memory of doing it. Anxiety arises because they're not sure if they've done it. In this case, anxiety is somewhat warranted (it's not *basic* anxiety). This *warranted* anxiety is intensified by high arousal, which produces an intense urge to repeat the task. But the major problem is the attention deficit. Simply *knowing* this might prompt the sufferer to pay special attention to the task, and with an audible or sub-audible voice, declare it done. It *might* work.

OCD sufferers with more basic anxiety: These sufferers may have fewer problems with second-by-second attention deficit, and more problems with *basic anxiety*. Some spiritual teachers recommend a method for dealing with basic anxiety. I have never applied this method. Apparently, the method involves holding your attention on the *feeling* of anxiety, which prevents your thoughts from creating a story that nurtures this anxiety. In time, the basic anxiety can be transcended. Would this method work with OCD symptoms? It may depend on how much *basic anxiety* is causing the symptoms.

If you need more information regarding this method, please consult a reputable source.

I have written many things in this book about the brain and mind. I have maintained that the functional link between these disorders is high arousal. This is a factor of the brain. My understanding regarding the *brain* was facilitated by:

- My strong ability to reason.
- The extra smooth crossover of symptoms of the three disorders.
- My slowness with reading and similar tasks.
- Disability concessions allowed me to study psychology.
- My continuous failure to hold jobs.

My understanding regarding the *mind* was facilitated

by episodes of darkness and practising presence. Both were necessary.

My episodes of darkness dissolved after five years of practising presence. I've been practising for nine years now. I've explained my experience with practising presence, but I have not provided much information on *how* to practise. I've now decided to provide some of that information. (For tips on practising presence, see Appendix D.)

Appendix A

Obsessive-Compulsive Disorder (OCD)

Obsessive-compulsive disorder (OCD) is a common, chronic, and long-lasting disorder in which a person has uncontrollable, reoccurring thoughts ("obsessions") and/or behaviours ("compulsions") that he or she feels the urge to repeat over and over.

Signs and Symptoms

People with OCD may have symptoms of obsessions, compulsions, or both. These symptoms can interfere with all aspects of life, such as work, school, and personal relationships.

Obsessions are repeated thoughts, urges, or mental images that cause anxiety. Common symptoms include:

- Fear of germs or contamination
- Unwanted forbidden or taboo thoughts involving sex, religion, or harm
- Aggressive thoughts towards others or self
- Having things symmetrical or in a perfect order

Compulsions are repetitive behaviours that a person with OCD feels the urge to do in response to an obsessive thought. Common compulsions include:

- Excessive cleaning and/or handwashing
- Ordering and arranging things in a particular, precise way
- Repeatedly checking on things, such as repeatedly checking to see if the door is locked or that the oven is off
- Compulsive counting

Not all rituals or habits are compulsions. Everyone double checks things sometimes. But a person with OCD generally:

- Can't control his or her thoughts or behaviours, even when those thoughts or behaviours are recognised as excessive.
- Spends at least one hour a day on these thoughts or behaviours.
- Doesn't get pleasure when performing the behaviours or rituals but may feel brief relief from the anxiety the thoughts cause.
- Experiences significant problems in their daily life due to these thoughts or behaviours.

Some individuals with OCD also have a tic disorder. Motor tics are sudden, brief, repetitive movements, such as eye blinking and other eye movements, facial grimacing, shoulder shrugging, and head or shoulder jerking. Common vocal tics include repetitive throat-clearing, sniffing, or grunting sounds.

Symptoms may come and go, ease over time, or worsen. People with OCD may try to help themselves by avoiding situations that trigger their obsessions, or they may use alcohol or drugs to calm themselves. Although most adults with OCD recognise that what they are doing doesn't make sense, some adults and most children may not realise that their behaviour is out of the ordinary. Parents or teachers typically recognise OCD symptoms in children.

If you think you have OCD, talk to your health care provider about your symptoms. If left untreated, OCD can interfere in all aspects of life.

Source: National Institute of Mental Health at:
https://www.nimh.nih.gov/health/topics/obsessive-compulsive-disorder-ocd

Appendix B

Attention Deficit Hyperactivity Disorder (ADHD)

Attention deficit hyperactivity disorder (ADHD) is a neurodevelopmental disorder (a problem related to brain development) that causes hyperactivity, impulsive behaviour, and attention problems. It interferes with a person's ability to exercise age-appropriate control of their behaviour and/or their cognition.

Children at school with ADHD may be seen as disruptive, they may tend to call out in class and appear not to listen to their teacher, they may also have difficulties keeping up with their peers academically. At home and in social situations they may do silly, irresponsible, or inappropriate things and they may seem to not respond to attempts to discipline them.

The child with ADHD is not wilfully naughty and their inability to be a good student or behave appropriately can be extremely distressing for them. Adults can have ADHD too and in their working life they may be seen as careless, inefficient employees. ADHD is the most common problem encountered in outpatient child and adolescent mental health settings and is 10 times more common in boys than in girls. Three types of ADHD are now recognised: predominantly inattentive type, predominantly hyperactive-impulsive type, and combined type.

Symptoms of inattention include:

- failing to complete activities or being slow to complete them
- not following through on instructions
- making careless mistakes
- having trouble organising activities
- frequently switching between activities
- being easily distracted and forgetful.

Symptoms of hyperactivity include:

- excessively active behaviour
- inappropriately running and climbing
- frequently leaving their seat
- fidgeting and squirming in their seat
- excessive talking
- being unable to play or work quietly
- even just subjective feelings of restlessness.

Symptoms of impulsivity include:

- difficulty awaiting their turn
- interrupting conversations and calling out
- generally acting without thinking.

Specific symptoms will vary from person to person, but a significant number must be present for behaviour to be seen as abnormal. Children or adults with predominantly inattentive type ADHD tend to be less obvious, they are often quiet, underachieving students who don't necessarily attract a lot of attention. Those who have symptoms of impulsivity and hyperactivity are much harder to overlook. Other important factors that define ADHD are that the symptoms occur in two or more settings (e.g., school and home), that symptoms were present before the age of 7 years, and that symptoms cause significant impairment in everyday functioning.

Studies suggest that the prevalence of ADHD has more than doubled in the last 10 years. This is partly because of an increased awareness and recognition of the disorder, but to some extent it is also because of misdiagnosis and the diagnostic criteria for ADHD not always being applied as rigorously as they should be. In addition to the ADHD characteristics listed above, many people with ADHD also show symptoms of other behavioural/psychiatric conditions that complicate the clinical picture, such as learning disabilities, anxiety, and disruptive behaviour disorders.

Source: Healthdirect Australia at:
https://www.healthdirect.gov.au/attention-deficit-disorder-add-or-adhd

Appendix C

Tourette Syndrome (TS)

What is Tourette Syndrome?

Tourette Syndrome, or TS, is an inherited neurological disorder that causes people to make involuntary and uncontrollable vocal sounds and movements, called tics.

Tourette Syndrome usually begins between 2 and 21 years of age.

There is no cure for TS, but it usually improves as the person gets older and does not shorten life span. Some people find the tics go away as they enter adulthood.

What are the symptoms of Tourette Syndrome?

Tourette Syndrome symptoms are usually mild but can sometimes be severe.

One set of symptoms is known as movement tics. People with movement tics can find themselves jerking their head, stretching their neck, stamping their feet, and twisting and bending. Some people may bite themselves or hurt themselves in other ways or find it necessary to repeatedly touch other people and things.

Another set of symptoms is known as vocal tics. People with vocal tics might clear their throat, cough, sniff, click their tongue, grunt, yelp, bark, or shout. Some also swear or repeat certain sounds or phrases.

Someone with Tourette Syndrome might be able to stop their tics for a short time, but this builds up tension until the tic escapes.

Tics worsen with stress and improve with relaxation or when the person is absorbed in a particular activity.

Tourette Syndrome can be accompanied by other conditions, such as attention deficit hyperactivity disorder (ADHD) and obsessive-compulsive disorder (OCD).

Tourette Syndrome doesn't affect anyone's intelligence.

How is Tourette Syndrome diagnosed?

To diagnose Tourette Syndrome, a doctor will talk about the symptoms and rule out that they're being caused by an illness or by medicine.

Living with Tourette Syndrome

Tourette Syndrome can cause problems with daily life, including learning, behaviour and sleep problems, anxiety, and mood changes.

Treatment for Tourette Syndrome uses medicine to reduce particular symptoms, though most people with Tourette Syndrome don't need treatment or medicine. Relaxation techniques can help reduce stress.

Source: Healthdirect Australia at:
https://www.healthdirect.gov.au/tourette-syndrome

Appendix D

Tips for Practising Presence

Beginning the practice: In the beginning, it may be better to choose a meditation technique that is easy for you. And it's good to attend a group where a coach can guide you. However, you will also need to practise at home.

Practising presence involves concentration, and it is common for beginners to lose concentration. It's important to expect this and to smile when it happens. Your smile is also part of your concentration. Once you smile, you can return to the major object of your concentration. There are many objects that practitioners can concentrate on. I will name some of the conventional ones:

1. There is walking meditation, where you feel your feet or your posture as you walk.

2. There is breathing meditation where you watch your inbreath and outbreath.

3. There are things you can do when you sit. For example, you can concentrate on relaxing your body. Some practitioners relax their forehead, then face, neck, shoulders, and they work their way down their body. Eventually, the whole body is relaxed (except the muscles used to sit upright).

I believe beginners should include "relaxation" with

all their meditation techniques. This stops you from trying too hard. I think that's important.

You can also concentrate on mantras. Mantras involve repeating words and concentrating on their pronunciation. You can sound the words under your breath. Or you can do it in an audible way if you practise by yourself. Remember to relax your muscles before you start a mantra (and maintain your relaxation). Mantras are useful in the early stages of your practice. They can give you an insight into concentration itself. For example, you can divide your concentration on the various syllables and find your own way. You can use an instructor to help you understand things but always study your own experience. Remember, meditation is about understanding.

Practitioners may want to use different techniques as they progress. They may eventually develop a technique that provides access to continuous presence. Watch videos, read books and talk to experts, and judge everything through your own experience. And be willing to change direction as you gain more experience.

Practising presence will help to dissolve the habit of overthinking. Overthinking is a habit that eventually causes suffering. Having a job that requires your full concentration may prevent overthinking, but this is like dwelling in a shelter. You won't learn to be aware of harmful thoughts. This is why you need to concentrate on tasks that do *not* require your full attention. This improves your awareness of your thoughts. They call it "being awake", as opposed to "daydreaming".

Quite often, practitioners are not ready for this practice, and may not persist with it. They may have difficulty understanding it. This is because their mind may not be dysfunctional enough. A dysfunctional mind causes suffering, which provides the opportunity to understand.

For the sake of people with high arousal: The practice does not require a memory. Therefore, people with high arousal should not have a problem with practising presence. However, some teachers incorporate memory activities into their practices. In the early stages of my practice, I was with a group that went around a circuit that had different meditation activities to do. I couldn't do it because I couldn't remember the activities. If I remember correctly, all the other participants could do it. These kinds of practices are not suitable for people with high arousal.

I mentioned above that people with high arousal should not have a problem with practising presence. However, people with OCD probably will. But this doesn't mean they shouldn't practise. Practising presence may be especially good for people with OCD, but they may need to include the method for dissolving basic anxiety (see Chapter 15).

How I developed my practice: In the beginning, I set aside a time for practice. After a while, I practised with less effort (i.e., relaxation). There were times when I'd meditate for two hours in bed. I'd do this when I wasn't likely to fall asleep. I would start with a mantra, which fine-tuned my concentration. After a while, I'd stop the mantra and concentrate on watching my breath. I eventually entered a very relaxed state. There were a couple times that my breathing became so faint that it almost stopped. These were incredible experiences. But I still experienced episodes of darkness in my life. I came to understand that it wasn't important to have these incredible experiences. Rather it was more important to heal my mind. Therefore, I needed to be present all the time. That's what I thought. And my intent was to achieve that.

I increased my practice, but I still had episodes of darkness. This failure didn't stop me from believing in the practice. I practised more and gained more understanding about it. My episodes of darkness dissolved after five years of practice. Four more years have passed since then, and I've gained more understanding. *Understanding* is important.

Understanding: As I said above, watch videos, read books, talk to experts, and judge everything through your own experience. You may encounter contradictions. Contradictions may be due to immature teachers, or our interpretation of their teaching. Be aware that different teachers may have different meanings for the same word. This is why I explained my meaning of the word: mind (see Chapter 15).

The most interesting thing I learnt was that *wanting* can block the progress. Even *wanting to progress on the path* can block it. So how do we progress? I will explain this in the next paragraph.

We all experience negative emotions. That is, our mind fears loss in the future, and/or it resents loss from the past. However, if we accept our fears and resentments, we can remove these attachments (bit by bit). Removing attachments is not about removing the thing we are attached to. It's about removing our attachment to it. Even when we practise, we may still fail to do this. But if we continue to practise, we can slowly remove our attachments. This is how we transcend the mind.

To learn more about Geoff,
please visit his website at:

geoffkanofski.com

www.ingramcontent.com/pod-product-compliance
Lightning Source LLC
LaVergne TN
LVHW011956070526
838202LV00054B/4937